HAYES

HARLINGTON

1939-1945

Published April 2005

With thanks to Pat and John Dando
for their interest and encouragement

Also in this series:-

Acknowledgements

In preparing this booklet I acknowledge the kind assistance given to me by the
following:-

Ken Pearce, Archivist, Bishopshalt School.
The Commonwealth War Graves Commission.
The Nationals Archives, Kew.
Mrs. S.A. Dickinson, The Ministry of Defence, Air Historical Branch (RAF), RAF
Bentley Priory, Stanmore.
Office for National Statistics, Family Records Office, Islington.
Royal Air Force Personnel Management Agency, Innsworth, Gloucester.
Fleet Air Arm Museum, Yeovilton.

and especially

The Libraries of the London Borough of Hillingdon

Artwork:- Carol Morgan

Hayes and Harlington

April 2005

Lest We Forget

They shall not grow old,
As we that are left grow old,
Age shall not weary them,
Nor the years condemn,
At the going down of the sun,
And in the morning,
We will remember them.

I have used the Memorials in St. Mary's, Hayes, and St. Peter's and St. Paul's, Harlington, and the records of the Commonwealth War Graves Commission to identify the servicemen and women of Hayes and Harlington who died in the Second World War.

This has shown 346 individuals which with the following,

198 for Ruislip, Northwood and Eastcote,
198 for Uxbridge, Ickenham, Harefield,
138 for West Drayton Yiewsley and Harmondsworth,

completes the details of all the 880 servicemen and servicewomen of the London Borough of Hillingdon who fell in the Second World War.

With Hayes and Harlington I have not been able to trace 12.
If anyone can provide any further information on these, it may be possible to include them in a reprint.
If any individuals are missing it is probably because the Commonwealth War Graves Commission's records are not complete.   This is usually-
a) because the Next of Kin and their addresses have not been included on their details.
b) their deaths fell outside the parameters of the C.W.G.C. (e.g. died in Canada in 1948, as was the case of a serviceman recorded on the Harefield Memorial).

The average age of the casualties of Hayes and Harlington was 26.

I have not included the civilian casualties of Hillingdon because they are covered by the Civilian Casualty Book, of which the Central Library in Uxbridge has a photo-copy, or is on the C.W.G.C. website.

ABBOTT Henry Thomas Abbott DSM

Leading Seaman C/J97368 H.M.S. *Avenger*, Royal Navy, who died on Sunday, 15th. November, 1942 aged 39.

He was the son of Robert A. and Elizabeth M. Abbott; husband of Harriet Beatrice Abbott; of Hayes. H.M.S. *Avenger* was an Escort Carrier of the *Archer* class, displacing 11500 tons and converted from a merchant ship's hull. She was the first of her type to be built, carried 16 aircraft, and had a crew of 565. The little ship had already proved her worth many times on the Russian convoys.

Her sinking was perhaps the most serious loss suffered by the Royal Navy in the North African landings. She was returning to the U.K. covering convoy MKF 1 when at 0414 hrs. she was torpedoed by U. 155. The torpedo caused a sympathetic detonation of the carrier's bomb room and she sank very quickly. There were only 12 survivors who were rescued by H.M.S. *Glendale* after spending some time in the water. This took place in the Atlantic just west of Gibraltar.

He was awarded the Distinguished Service Medal which was gazetted posthumously on the 1st. December, 1942.

He is commemorated on the Chatham Naval Memorial Panel 52.1, and St. Mary's, Hayes.

ABLEY Philip Kenneth

Leading Aircraftman 908333 Royal Air Force Volunteer Reserve, who died on Friday, 1st. November, 1940 aged 19.

He was the son of Harold E. and Elizabeth Abley, of Hayes.

He was attached to No. 8. Service Flying Training School at Montrose, Scotland, training to be a pilot. He was flying a Miles Master single engined advance trainer with pupil and instructor in tandem when he had an accident, and crashed at Johnshaven, north of Montrose,

He is buried at Merthyr Tydfil (Aberfan) Cemetery, Glamorgan. Row N. Grave 19.

ACOURT Richard George

Private 5731222 2nd. Battalion, Dorsetshire Regiment, who died on Tuesday, 20th. March, 1945 aged 24.

He was the son of Robert E. and Mary A. Acourt, of Hayes End.

The 2nd. Battalion was part of the 5th. Infantry Brigade of the 2nd. (British) Infantry Division who had crossed the Chindwin river and were now advancing in Central Burma. General *Slim*'s plan was to cut off Mandalay from Rangoon at Meiktila, on the river Irrawaddy. Mandalay was captured on the 21st. and Richard died in this battle. The Japanese then commenced their retreat and by July had left Burma and were retreating in Siam, when the dropping of the two Atom bombs ended the war.

He is buried at Taukkyan War Cemetery, Myanmar, (Burma). Grave 17. E. 10, and commemorated at St. Mary's Hayes.

ALDRIDGE William Richard

Gunner 14334834 191 (The Hertfordshire and Essex Yeomanry) Field Regiment, Royal Artillery, who died on Saturday, 17th. July, 1943 aged 19.

He was the son of William A. and Margaret D. Aldridge, of Dunbar Close, Hayes.

He died at the Military Families Hospital, South Tidworth, Wilts. of injuries sustained when the Armoured O. P. Truck in which he was travelling overturned at Tidworth.

He is buried at Hayes and Harlington (Cherry Lane) Cemetery. Sec. C.2. Grave H.8

NOTE

Between 1940 and 1945 the training was so realistic and difficult, that ten percent of all soldiers were either injured or killed.

ANDREWS Charles Ernest

Craftsman 10545989 Royal Electrical and Mechanical Engineers, who died on Tuesday, 22nd. December, 1942 aged 31.

He was the son of Charles and Emily E. Andrews, of Hayes.

He was a passenger on the liner *Srathallan*. She was a P. & O. steamship of 24,000 tons built by Vickers in 1938 and had a speed of 21 knots. She left the Clyde on December, 11th. for Algiers with 4,408 troops and 248 nurses on board. At 0230 hrs. on the 21st. she was hit by two torpedoes from the U. 562 about 40 miles north of Oran. Fire broke out in the engine room and spread to a hold containing ammunition. Charles, a few passengers and six of the crew were killed, including Leonard **BIGGS,** a gunner from Hayes. The remainder were taken off by the escorts and a salvage tug took the ship in tow, but she sank 12 miles from Oran at 0420 hrs. on the 22nd.

He is buried at La Reunion War Cemetery, Algeria. Grave 5. B. 14. and commemorated at St. Mary's Hayes. This cemetery is 250 kms. east of Algiers.

ANDREWS Sydney Ernest   D.F.M.

Flying Officer 44567 R.A.F. who died on Sunday, 9th. August, 1942.

He lived in Orchard Road, Hayes.

He was a pilot attached to No.3 (Middle East) Aircraft Repair Unit based at Ismailia in the Canal Zone. He was flying a Curtiss Tomahawk single-engined fighter when he crashed at 1100 hrs. at Moascar which is a mile from Ismailia. He was awarded the Distinguished Flying Medal on the 5th. November,1940, for outstanding service when flying Fairey Battle Light Bombers with 150 Squadron in France and from R.A.F. Newton, which is east of Nottingham.

He is buried at Ismailia War Memorial Cemetery, Egypt. Grave 7. B. 9. Ismailia is a small town on the west side of the Suez Canal and contains 291 Second World War burials. He is commemorated at Bishopshalt School where he was a former pupil.

APLIN Donald Percy

Sergeant 1891334 R.A.F.V.R. who died on Thursday, 8th. February, 1945.

He was a Flight Engineer flying Lancaster 111s with 57 Squadron, of 5 Group based at East Kirkby, Lincs.

They took off at 1703 hrs. to attack a synthetic oil production plant at Politz, Poland. They were hit by anti-aircraft fire after entering Swedish air space and crashed on farmland at Brohult near Hjortshog. The pilot survived and was interned but the other six airmen, including Donald died and are buried at Helsingborg (Palsjo) Municipal Cemetery, Sweden, Section XV. His grave is 84A.

He is commemorated at St. Mary's, Hayes. Also flying in this aircraft was Flight Sergeant **Edward C. SLAUGHTER** (see below) an Air Bomber also from Hayes, who also died. They were probably close friends and they lie in adjoining graves.

"And in their death, they were not divided".

Also buried in this cemetery is Sergeant **William R. CAMPBELL** of 50 Squadron who died on the 30th August, 1944.

484 aircraft were despatched and 12 failed to return. The raid was a complete success, and the plant did not produce any more oil for the rest of the war.

ARNOLD Ivor James

Private 6098763 2nd. Battalion, The Hertfordshire Regiment, Bedfordshire and Hertfordshire Regiment, who died on Tuesday, 16th. May, 1944, aged 24.

He was the son of George and Caroline R. Arnold, of Hayes.

The 2nd. Battalion was part of the 10th. Infantry Brigade of the 4th. Infantry Division (British not the famous 4th. Indian) who served in North Africa from 25th. March to the 15th December, 1943.

2

They moved to Egypt and then arrived in Italy on the 21st. February, 1944. They were now taking part in Operation *Diadem*, the attempt to take Monte Cassino and breach the *Gustav Line* in which they succeeded.

Ivor died on the day that *Kesselring* decided to abandon the Gustav Line and flee northwards to Rome. He is buried at Cassino War Cemetery, Italy Grave X11. G.7, and commemorated at St. Peter's and St. Paul's, Harlington

The D-Day Dodgers

(to the tune of Lili Marlene)

Oh, We're the D-Day dodgers, out in Italy,
Always on the vino, always on the spree
Eighth Army scroungers, and with our tanks
We live in Rome, amongst the Yanks
We are the D-Day dodgers in sunny Italy.

We landed at Salerno, a holiday with pay
The Jerries brought the bands out to greet us on our way
Showed us the sights and gave us tea
We all sang songs, the beer was free
To welcome D-Day dodgers to sunny Italy.

Naples and Cassino were taken in our stride
We didn't come to fight here, we just came for the ride
Anzio and Sangro were just names
We only came looking for the dames
The randy D-Day dodgers in sunny Italy.

On the way to Florence we had a lovely time
We ran a bus to Rimini, right through the Gothic line
Soon to Bologna we will go
and after that we'll cross the Po
We'll still be D-Day dodging in sunny Italy.

Dear Lady Astor, you think you know a lot
Standing on your platform and talking tommyrot
You, England's sweetheart and its pride
We think your mouth's too bleedin' wide
That's from your D-Day Dodgers in sunny Italy.

Look around the mountains in the mud and rain
See the scattered crosses, there's some that have no names
Heartache and sorrow are all gone
The boys beneath them slumber on
They are the D-Day dodgers who'll stay in Italy.

Voices in the UK, possibly inspired by Lady Astor MP, implied that the troops left in Italy to battle their way northwards had taken the easy option.

3

ASHFIELD Edward William

Corporal 335254 R.A.F. who died on Tuesday, 3rd. November, 1942 aged 40.

He was the son of Edwin W. and Agnes Ashfield; husband of Lilian Elizabeth Ashfield, of Hayes.

He was serving with 651 Squadron flying Auster 1 single-engined, artillery spotting planes based at Gourock. They were about to go to Tunis to join First Army in Operation Torch, the campaign to drive the Germans and Italians out of Algeria and Tunisia.

He was involved in a road traffic accident at Kidsdale and was admitted to the EMS Hospital, Galloway House, Garleston where he died of his injuries.

He is buried at Glasserton Parish Churchyard, Wigtownshire. Sec. D. Grave 3.

ASHWORTH Ernest William

Second Engineer, S.S. *River Lugar* (Glasgow), Merchant Navy, who died on Thursday, 26th. June, 1941 aged 54.

He was the son of James W. and Dorothy Ashworth (nee Smollett); husband of Frances Louisa Ashworth, of Hayes.

The *River Lugar* was a steamship of 5,500 tons, built in 1937 and owned by Ayrshire Navigation. She was on a voyage from Pepel to Barry Roads, South Wales, with 9,250 tons of iron ore, when she was torpedoed and sunk by U. 69, 1100 miles west of Freetown. The U boat had aimed for another ship, but missed and hit the *River Lugar*. Thirty-nine of her crew (including Ernest) and two passengers were lost. Six survivors were picked up some time later.

He is commemorated on the Tower Hill Memorial. Panel 87.

ASHWORTH Frank

Sergeant 517396 Pilot R.A.F. who died on Saturday, 24th. May, 1941.

He was the son of Solomon and Susannah R. Ashworth; husband of Hilda Mary Ashworth, of Hayes.

He was a pilot instructor at No.24 Elementary Flying School and was a flying a Miles Magister single engined trainer which had the pupil and instructor in tandem. The aircraft crashed at Shillinton. Beds. (near Luton) and Frank was killed.

He is buried at Hayes and Harlington (Cherry Lane) Cemetery. Sec. C.1. Grave R.27.

ATKINS Frederick

Private 6141606 2nd. Battalion, East Surrey Regiment, who died on Saturday, 7th February, 1942 aged 23.

He was the son of J. H. and May Atkins, of Hayes,

In 1939 the Battalion was stationed in Shanghai, China and moved to Malaya in September 1940 to join the 1st. Malaya Brigade. The Japanese invaded Malaya on the 8th. December, 1941 and the Surreys and the 1st. Leicesters suffered heavy casualties in early December and were amalgamated to form the British Battalion of the 15th. Indian Infantry Brigade. The Japanese crossed the causeway from Malaya to Singapore on the 31st. January, 1941. Stanley died in the final battles for Singapore before the Allies surrendered on the 15th, February, 1942.

He is commemorated on the Singapore Memorial, Column 68.

BABER Stanley Ernest

Sergeant 1338704 R. A. F. V. R. who died on Tuesday, 31st. August, 1943 aged 21.

He was the son of Ernest S. and Edith L. Baber, of Hayes.

He was Air Bomber flying Wellington X s with 166 Squadron of 1 Group, based at Kirmington, Lincs., (just south of Hull). They took off at 0042 hrs. to attack Munchengladbach and Rheyt. Six hundred and sixty aircraft were despatched. It was a double attack on the two towns and the "Oboe" marking was excellent (transmission of radio beams from ground stations to give bombing position).

About half the built-up area in each town was destroyed. They were lost without trace with 44 other aircraft. All five crew were killed, and all were aged under 22. They are all commemorated on the Runnymede Memorial. Panel 141, and Stanley is also commemorated at St. Mary's, Hayes.

BACON James Edward

Flight Sergeant 907761 R.A.F.V.R. who died on Tuesday, 14th. July, 1942 aged 22.
He was the son of Thomas J. and Kate E. Bacon, of Hayes End. and the brother of Thomas (see below). who had been killed three months earlier.
He was a Wireless Operator / Air Gunner flying Catalina 111a s with 119 Squadron based at Lough Erne, Northern Island, but was on detachment to Pembroke Docks, Wales. The Catalina was an American twin engined ocean flying boat with a crew of eight, and a very long range. His aircraft went missing, presumed lost at sea due to enemy action.
He is commemorated on the Runnymede Memorial. Panel 73, and St. Mary's, Hayes.

BACON Thomas John

Sergeant 755229 R.A.F.V.R. who died on Tuesday, 14th. April, 1942 aged 26.
He was a navigator flying Beaufort 1 s twin engined torpedo bombers with 39 Squadron based at Landing Ground 86, south of Alexandria, Egypt.
A large Axis convoy was making its way south from Italy to Libya. Twelve Beauforts, including 2 from 22 Squadron proceeded to Sidi Barrani where the crews were briefed and sent to Bu Amud to stand by. They took off at noon, flew in a straight line to find the convoy of 4 motor vessels and 6 destroyers. The Beaufighter escort of 4 aircraft returned to base due to lack of fuel. Eight torpedoes were dropped but because of the very large escort of fighters four Beauforts were lost, including Thomas's.
One newspaper reporter went into a barrack room in Malta where the Sergeant navigators of the Beauforts were billeted. and noted there were twenty two. He returned two weeks later and there were only three, such was the heavy losses suffered by them.
He is commemorated on the Alamein Memorial, Column 250, and St. Mary's Hayes.

BAISDEN Alexander Victor

Gunner 6734805 1 Airlanding Light Regiment, Royal Artillery, who died on Sunday, 24th. September, 1944 aged 28.
He was the son of Norman A. and Rebecca Baisden; husband of Eileen Violet Baisden, of Hayes.
He is buried at Arnhem Oosterbeek War Cemetery, Gelderland, Holland. Grave 6. A. 6.

To avoid repetition overleaf there is a short note on the Battle of Arnhem overleaf.

The following also died in this operation.
Robert H, Burton
Leonard S. Harper
Edwin H. Lascelles
Albert Law
David McMahon

5

Operation Market Garden - The Bridge at Arnhem
17th. to 25th. September 1944

The Allied plans were to insert three airborne divisions behind enemy lines to seize eight bridges in Holland over which the British Second Army would advance, thus outflanking the *Siegfried* Line. The American 101st. Airborne Division (Screaming Eagles, See "Band of Brothers") would take the Eindhoven bridge, and the 82nd Airborne Division (All American), Nijmegen and the British 1st.. Airborne Division, Arnhem. This was to pave the way for the capture of the Ruhr and end the war in just a few months. They thought the German forces were very weak but underestimated the experience and skill of the German defenders.

Sunday the 17th. September, just after 2.00 p.m. some 20,000 combat troops, 511 vehicles, 330 artillery pieces, and 600 tons of equipment had been safely landed. At Arnhem by nightfall John Frost's 2nd. Battalion held the north side of the road bridge.

Operation *Garden*, the land forces advance had also been launched. but XXX Corps had been held up by the Germans blowing up the bridge at Son, despite the effort of the 101st. to capture it. More German re-inforcements were introduced at Arnhem and the British felt they were being surrounded. But by evening the Guards had reached Son and were building a temporary Bailey bridge over the river.

Tuesday there was more bad news when the weather prevented re-inforcements being sent into Arnhem. The British were concentrating around the Hartenstein Hotel and 2 Para were still isolated at the bridge. It was now clear to Frost that 2 Para would not be reinforced by the rest of the Division but would have to wait for the ground troops advancing from the south

They had reached Grave and the 82nd. Airborne were now preparing an assault with boats on the bridge at Nijmegen. With increasing pressure the British 1st. Airborne's commander Urquhart decided on the 20th. to defend a thumb shaped perimeter at Oosterbeck. with its base on the river. The leading tanks crossed the Waal that night after the successful assault by the 82nd Airborne, they could see the smoke rising from Arnhem. But although only eight miles away without infantry support the exhausted Guards Armoured stopped for the night.

Fighting continued on the 21st. September but gradually petered out and the Airborne troops at Arnhem were overrun. With the bridge now open the Germans raced across and set up defensive positions, to halt XXX Corps. The 1st. Polish Parachute brigade were dropped, unfortunately south of the river at Arnhem. On the 22nd. XXX Corps linked up with them.

On the 24/25th. Operation *Berlin*, the evacuation of the 1st.Airborne at Arnhem over the river took place. At Arnhem, 1485 Allied troops had been killed, 3,910 had been evacuated, and 6525 had been taken prisoner, of whom 2,250 were wounded. The British casualties were twice as heavy as the Americans.

BAKER Albert

Private 4807634 1st. Battalion, West Yorkshire Regiment, (Prince of Wales Own) who died on Sunday, 12th. March, 1944 aged 30.

He was the son of James and Selina Baker; husband of Ellen Lilian Baker, of Hayes.

In mid March 1943 the Japanese began their offensive in Imphal and Kohima as the first step in the invasion of India. General *Slim* gave orders for the troops to pull back from the outlying areas and concentrate in the Plain of Imphal, making it easier to supply by air and lengthening the Japanese lines of communication. Albert died in these preliminary actions.

When a British soldier died in the jungle he was buried and an officer made a note in the Company records of the map reference so that he could be reburied at a later date. Unfortunately this was not always possible and in Albert's case he is commemorated on the Rangoon Memorial, Myanmar, (Burma). Face 7.

BALDWIN William Charles
Gunner 6459432 12 Coast Regiment, Royal Artillery, who died on the 1st. October, 1942 aged 22.
He was the son Elisa J. Baldwin of Hayes.
He was taken prisoner by the Japanese when Hong Kong fell on the 26th. December, 1941.
He was then being moved to Japan on the Liner *Lisbon Maru*, when she was torpedoed and sunk by the U.S. Submarine *Grouper*.
Please see Ronald **Bath** for the rest of the details.
He is commemorated on the Sai Wan Memorial, Hong Kong. Column 3.

BALL William Frederick
Gunner 6205587 118 Field Regiment, Royal Artillery, who died on Sunday 27th. June, 1943 aged 23.
He was the son of Alfred F. and Gertrude Ball, of 104. Berwick Avenue, Hayes.   He was a Fitter's improver in civilian life.   The Japanese records state that he was Frederick William, and the Commonweath War Graves records just state he was W.F.
The 118 Field Regiment was part of the 18th. Infantry Division which was switched from the Middle East to Malaya in December 1941 and arrived just before the surrender of Singapore on February, 15th, 1942. (Please see note after **Gerald GREEN**).   He was sent to work on the Burma-Siam railway and died in captivity from the dreadful conditions.
He is buried at Kanchanaburi War Cemetery, Siam Sp. Mem. 9. M.4, and commemorated at St. Mary's Hayes.

The Burma-Siam Railway

The notorious Burma-Siam Railway, built by Commonwealth, Dutch and American prisoners of war, was a Japanese project driven by the need for improved communications to support their large army in Burma.   During its construction, approximately 13,000 P.O.W.s died and were buried along the railway.   An estimated 80,000 to 100,000 civilians also died on this project, chiefly forced labour brought in from Malaya and the Dutch East Indies, Siam, and Burma.   Two labour forces one based in Siam and Burma worked from opposite ends of the line towards the centre.   Work began in October, 1942 and the line 424 kilometres long was completed by December, 1943.   The graves of those who died during construction were transferred from the isolated areas to three cemeteries at Chungkai and Kanchanaburi in Thailand and Thanbyuzayat in Burma.
The railway was repeatedly bombed by the Allied Air Forces in 1944/1945.

BAMBER Harry John
Flight Lieutenant 10220 R.A.F. who died on Friday, 9th. May, 1941 aged 51.
He was serving in the Station Headquarters at RAF Cranwell, Lincs.   He died in an accident (no other details given).
He is buried at Hayes and Harlington (Cherry Lane) Cemetery. Sec. C.1. Grave R.17.

BANKS R.
Although commemorated at St. Mary's, Hayes, unfortunately I have not been able to trace this person

BARKER William Charles
Private 14804826 1st. Battalion, The Queen's Royal Regiment, (West Surrey) who died on Friday, 27th. July, 1945 aged 19.
He was the son of William C. and Emily V. Barker, of Hayes.

The 1st. Battalion was part of the 33rd. Indian Infantry Brigade of the 7th. Indian Infantry Division who had crossed the river Chindwin in February 1945 to recapture Burma. Mandalay had fallen on the 21st. March, 1945 and they were advancing up the river Irrawaddy to liberate Rangoon. They were switched from this advance to the river Sittang to the east to prevent 60,000 Japanese troops escaping first to Siam and then to Malaya..

20th. July was to be the D-Day for the breakout by the Japanese 29th. Army and they attempted for two weeks to cross the Rangoon-Mandalay road. "The Battle of the Breakout" was a disaster for the Japanese, costing them 11,000 killed and 4,000 missing. Unfortunately William died in this battle, one of the last, but it must be remembered that the Allies thought the war would go on to 1946 and it was vital to prevent these Japanese troops escaping to Malaya to fight another day. In early August the Americans dropped the two Atom bombs and the war in the East was over.

Although after most battle attempts were made to bury the dead it was not always possible to locate them and William is commemorated at the Rangoon Memorial, Face 4, and at St. Mary's, Hayes.

BARNES Frederick Charles

Corporal 531600 R.A.F. who died on Saturday, 18th. April, 1942 aged 29.

He was the son of Frederick C. and Mary Barnes; husband of Alma Doris Barnes, of Hayes. He was an aircraft chargehand on general duties with No. 80 Wing, Windlesham, Surrey. He was admitted to Cambridge Military Hospital on the 6th, dangerously ill and died 12 days later. He is buried at the Brookwood Military Cemetery, Surrey. Grave 21. B. 7.

BARNES George

Civilian who died on Thursday, 17th, April. 1941 aged 63.

He was the son of Mr. and Mrs. Barnes , of 13, Dorset Close, Hayes; husband of Charlotte Eliza Barnes.

He died in air raid at 3, Searle Street, where he was living and is buried at Battersea Metropolitan Borough Cemetery. He is commemorated at St. Mary's. Hayes.

BARROW Stanley Francis

Sergeant 1386172 R.A.F.V.R. who died on Thursday, 26th. May, 1943 aged 22.

He was a Wireless Operator / Air Gunner flying Wellington X s with 166 Squadron of 1 Group based at Kirmington, Lincs.

They took of at 2357 hrs. to attack Dusseldorf in the Ruhr. They were hit by flak and crashed at the hamlet of Prootstdijk, (Limburg). All five of the crew were killed and are buried at Eindhoven (Woensel) General Cemetery, Holland. Plot EE Collective Grave 34-35. He is commemorated at St. Mary's, Hayes.

759 aircraft were despatched to attack Dusseldorf but the raid was a failure. The bombing was scattered over a large area due to the Germans using decoy markers, and 27 aircraft were lost.

BASKERVILLE G.D.

Although commemorated at St. Mary's, Hayes, unfortunately I have not been able to trace this person

BASS Gordon John

Ordinary Seaman P/JX 275886 H.M.S. *Culver*, Royal Navy, who died on Saturday, 31st. January, 1942 aged 21.

He was the son of Ethelbert and Hilda M. Bass, of Drenon Square, Hayes, Middx. He was the elder brother of Raymond Lionel.

H.M.S. *Culver* was a Royal Navy Cutter (ex U.S. Coast Guard) built in 1929. She was escorting convoy SL.98 when she was attacked and sunk by U 105. The U 105 had fired a four torpedo spread at the convoy and they observed two hits and a big explosion. They first thought they had hit an ammunition ship but in fact two torpedoes hit the *Culver* which blew up with massive force. *Culver* had been fitted with an operational automatic High Frequency Direction finding set, but this had not saved her. The sinking took place south-west of Ireland.

He is commemorated at the Portsmouth Naval Memorial. Panel 65. Column 2, St. Mary's, Hayes, and Bishopshalt School where he was a former pupil.

BASS Raymond Lionel

Ordinary Seaman P/JX 794392, H.M.S. *Actaeon*, Royal Navy, who died on Friday, 20th. December, 1946 aged 19.

Younger brother of Gordon John.

H.M.S. *Action* was a sloop of 1850 tons displacement built in 1945 by Thornecrofts which survived the was and was sold to Germany in 1953 and renamed *Hipper*.

Raymond "died on war service" and was buried at sea.

He is commemorated at the Portsmouth Naval Memorial Panel 90. Column 2, and St. Mary's, Hayes.

BATH Ronald Jack

Private 6292182 1st. Battalion, Middlesex Regiment, who died on Thursday, 1st. October, 1942 aged 26.

He was the son of George and Emily Bath, of Hayes.

In the summer of 1939 the Battalion was preparing to go to Malta but this was cancelled when war broke out in September. In June 1940 all wives and dependants of married men were sent to Australia as a precaution. The regimental silver was sent to Singapore, where it was captured by the Japanese. It was however recovered, and returned to the regiment after the war.

On the 8th. December 1941 the Japanese attacked Hong Kong and on the 26th. December after fighting fiercely against large odds the garrison surrendered and marched into captivity.

After ten months of captivity at Shang Shui Po, a large draft of prisoners of war was ordered to a new camp in Japan, Eighteen hundred men, including the bulk of the 1st. Battalion, were taken on board the *Lisbon Maru* and accommodated in the hold.

"At 0700 hours on the 1st. October 1942. the ship was hit by a torpedo from the U.S. submarine *Grouper* and began to sink. When the majority of the Japanese had abandoned ship, leaving their prisoners battened down in the holds, Colonel Stewart, showing fine leadership, organised the forcing of the hatches. The first men out were fired on by the guards as they came on deck, but a great many escaped due to the example of Colonel Stewart. Yet in spite of all his efforts the loss of life was grievous and 133 men of the Battalion perished".

The above is from the Regimental History published in the fifties but another later source in the 1980s states that the Japanese rescue ships used the prisoners for target practice.

He is commemorated on the Sai Wan Memorial, Hong Kong, China. Column 14, and also at St. Mary's Hayes.

Please note William Baldwin, Alex Taylor of Hayes and Stanley Langdell of Northwood also died in this ship.

BAXTER John Cockburn   MM

Private 14203904 2/4th. Battalion, Hampshire Regiment, who died on Monday, 18th. December, 1944 aged 22.

He was the son of George and Sophia Robson Baxter, of Hayes.

The 2/4th. Battalion was part of the 2nd. Gibraltar Brigade of the 4th. (British) Infantry Division. who served in Italy from the 16th. March to the 11th. December, 1944 and had taken part in the advance from Cassino in the south to the Rimini Line.

On the 12th. December they were sent to Greece to combat the communist resistance *ELAS* who were marching to Athens to seize power. John died on the day that the 4th Indian Infantry Division arrived in Greece to reinforce them. On the 4th, January, 1945 the final battle took place and the *ELAS* forces withdrew from the city and commenced cease-fire negotiations.

He is buried at the Phaleron War Cemetery, Athens, Greece. Grave 18. A. 13, and commemorated at St. Mary's, Hayes.

The London Gazette 8th. February 1945

The King has been graciously pleased to approve the award of the Military Medal in recognition of his gallant and distinguished services in Italy.

BAXTER Montague Frank

Flying Officer 124108 R.A.F.V.R. who died on Monday, 22nd. November, 1943 aged 27.
He was the son of Frederick G. and Elizabeth E. Baxter, of Hayes.

He was a rear gunner flying Halifax 11 s with 10 Squadron of 4 Group based at Melbourne, Yorks. They took off at 1654 hrs. with 763 other bombers to attack Berlin. This was the largest force sent so far and this was the last raid when Stirlings were used. It was the most successful raid on Berlin of the war, and 175,000 people were bombed out of their dwellings. 26 aircraft were lost including Montague's. All seven crew were killed and are commemorated on the Runnymede Memorial. Panel 123.

BEALE Lionel Leonard

Gunner 943516 121 Field Regiment, Royal Artillery, who died on Friday, 14th. May, 1943 aged 24. He was the son of Leonard F. and Dorothy K. O. Beale; of Bourne Avenue; husband of Joan Louise Beale, of Hayes.

121 Field Regiment was part of the central artillery of XXX Corps, Eighth Army and he died as a result of wounds received in the final battle for Tunisia. The Axis surrendered on the 13th. May, 1943

He is buried at Enfidaville War Cemetery, Tunisia. Grave 1. B. 14. The town of Enfidaville is 100 kilometres south of Tunis on the main coast road. He is commemorated on the Memorials at St. Mary's, Hayes, St. Peter's and St. Paul's, Harlington, and Bishopshalt School where he was a former pupil.

BECK Albert

Private 6472230 1st. Battalion, King's Own Royal Regiment (Lancaster), who died on Saturday, 15th. July, 1944 aged 30,
He was the son of Bertie and Isabella Beck, of Hayes End.

The 1st. Battalion served in the Middle East as part of the Indian Army until Spring 1944. On the 14th. March. 1944 they amalgamated with the 8th. Battalion and moved to Italy as part of the 25th. Indian Infantry Brigade.

On the 15th. July they took part in the assault on the l'Olmo gap through which pass the road to the strategic stronghold of Arezzo on the River Arno in Tuscany. Albert died in the initial fighting but the Gap was forced, Arezzo fell on the 17th. and an intact bridge across the Arno had been seized to allow the advance to continue.

He is buried at Arezzo War Cemetery, Italy. Grave 1. B. 4, and is commemorated at St. Mary's, Hayes.

BEEBE Kenneth Charles
Gunner 1155384 25 Field Regiment, Royal Artillery, who died on Sunday, 16th. July, 1944 aged 20.
He was the son of William G. and Alice Baxter, of Hayes.
He is buried at St. Manvieu War Cemetery, Cheux, Calvados, Normandy. Grave X. H. 19.

Normandy The British and Canadian Sector 9-17th. July 1944

Although Caen had fallen on the 8th. the Allies were now suffering from German counter-attacks as more troops were brought in from the rest of France, and Europe. Fortunately they were being brought into the line on the Allied left flank and not opposing the Americans on the right. Kenneth died as did William **Horspool**, Terence **Lofts**, Edward **Russell**, and Stanley **Simpson**, defending the beachhead the Allies had achieved over the river Odon.

The British were now preparing for Operation *Goodwood*, the three armoured division attack to the east of Caen, which was only partially successful, and the Americans for Operation *Cobra* which was a complete success and led to the successful breakout from the beachhead.

The return to Europe The basic rations for the first two days.

Every soldier drew 200 francs in the new Liberation notes and a little handbook entitled "France", with a picture of the Arc de Triomphe on the front. They were issued with various novelties for their first "fend for themselves" hours ashore. They were the possessors of two "twenty-four hour packs", little packages containing dehydrated porridge, dehydrated meat, some four bars of chocolate and some chewing gum, for the first forty-eight house in France. Also included was a hexamite cooker heated by circular tablets two inches wide and half an inch deep - which when ignited by a match gave a very hot flame. They also had water-purifying tablets and a very fine pair of waterwings ??
It was however *Montgomery* and his commander's policy where ever possible to ensure that a soldier "has a hot meal before going into battle".

BENNETT James William Robert
Private 14219880 2nd. Special Service Regiment, Army Air Corps, who died on Monday, 16th. October, 1944 aged 20.
He was the son of James and Elizabeth A. Bennett, of Hayes.
According to his death certificate James was "presumed killed in action on the 10th. October, 1944". As the SAS records are still unreleased we have to try and imagine what happened. On the 10th. October the furthest east the Allies had advanced was Aachen, and they were now planning to clear the west bank, and cross the Rhine in December / January. He was probably sent behind enemy lines to reconnoitre the ground, was killed and buried locally.
After the war ended he would have been removed to Durnbach Cemetery which had been established to contain all the graves scattered across Germany, apart from those in the main cemeteries (e.g. Berlin, Kleve)
He is buried at Durnbach War Cemetery, Bad Tolz, Bayern, Germany. Grave 3. K. 4, and commemorated at St. Mary's, Hayes.

BENTON Douglas
Lieutenant 268240 Royal Corps of Signals, who died on Saturday, 31st. March, 1945 aged 25
He was the son of Herbert C. and Emma L. Benton, of Hayes.

11

At the end of 1944 the Allied Chiefs of Staff decided to transfer five divisions (20% of the Allied forces) from Italy to the North Western European front. Although in the end only two divisions were moved the Allied forces in Italy went on the defensive until April 1945.

But even in quiet periods soldiers get killed, and Douglas died of his wounds in a rare German attack. As he has no unit detailed, it is difficult to pinpoint the place where he died.

He is buried at Ravenna War Cemetery, Italy. Grave 1. A. 18. Ravenna is a northern city near the Adriatic.

BEYAN Stewart

Fusilier 4192813 1st. Battalion, Royal Welch Fusiliers, who died on Friday, 10th. May, 1940, aged 21.

He was the son of Llewelyn and Thurza Mary Beyan, of Hayes. Kindly note the Commonwealth War Graves Commission incorrectly lists him as **BEVAN**.

The 1st. Battalion was part of the 6th. Infantry Brigade of the 2nd, Infantry Division which was sent to France as part of the British Expeditionary Force on the 24th. September, 1939. On May 10th. the Germans launched their Blitzkrieg through the Ardennes. defeating the British and French and forcing them to evacuate through Dunkirk in late May.

Stewart's death certificate states he died between the 10th. May, 1940 and the 27th. February, 1941, but he was probably killed in May 1940 and his body found later in February, 1941.

He is buried at Lille Southern Cemetery, Nord, France. Grave Plot 5, Row D. Grave 11.

BIGGS Leonard Vincent

Gunner 1139039 Royal Artillery, who died on Monday, 21st. December, 1942 aged 19.

He was the son of Mr. and Mrs. A.J. Biggs, of Hayes.

He was a gunner on the liner *Srathallan*.

Please see Charles **Andrews** who was a passenger and also died in this ship.

He is commemorated on the Brookwood Memorial, Surrey. Panel 3 Column 1, and St. Mary's Hayes,

BINKS George Edward

Corporal, 5766292 4th. Battalion, Wiltshire Regiment, who died on Tuesday, 10th. October, 1944 aged 33.

He was the son of Edward and Emma Binks; husband of Ena May Binks, of Hayes.

The 4th. Battalion with the 5th. Wilts. and the 4th. Somersets formed the 129th. Infantry Brigade of the 43rd. Wessex Infantry Division. They had landed in Normandy on the 17th.June (D.Day + 11) and had advanced through France and Belgium. They had tried to link up with the paratroopers at Arnhem but had not succeeded. The Battle of Arnhem had ended on the 26th. September and George died defending the "Island", the land between the branches of the Rhine at Arnhem and Nijmegen from German counter-attacks.

He is buried at Jonkerbos War Cemetery, Gelderland, Holland. Grave 9, G, 1, and commemorated at St. Mary's, Hayes.

The London Gazette 10th. May, 1945

The King was graciously pleased to approve that the following be mentioned in recognition of his gallant and distinguished service in N.W. Europe.

Corporal G.E. Binks

BIRKS Aubrey
Fifth Engineer Officer M.V. *Surat* (London), Merchant Navy, who died on Tuesday, 6th. May, 1941 aged 25.
He was the son of Kate Birks, of Highgate, Middx.
The *Surat* was a motor vessel of 5500 tons and was torpedoed and sunk by the U. 103 off the coast of Gambia.
He is commemorated on the Tower Hill Memorial, Panel 104, and on the memorials at St. Mary's, Hayes and St. Peter's and St, Paul's, Harlington.

BLACKHAM Peter Douglas
Flying Officer 142196 R.A.F.V.R. who died on Saturday, 8th. July, 1944.
He was a pilot flying Lancaster 111 s with 9 Squadron of 5 Group based at Bardney, near Lincoln. They took off at 2245 hrs. tasked to attack a flying bomb depot in a group of tunnels at St. Le. d'Esserent, which had formerly been used to grow mushrooms. The bombing was accurately directed on to the mouth of the tunnels and the approach roads, thus blocking access to the flying bombs. Night fighters intercepted the force of 208 Lancasters and 13 Mosquitoes and 31 aircraft were lost, including Peter's. Six of the crew were killed but the Flight Engineer, Sgt. Massie parachuted to safety and evaded capture.
Peter is buried at Ecquevilly Communal Cemetery, Yvelines, France (south-east of Mantes). Grave 5, and commemorated at St. Mary's, Hayes, and St. Peter's and St. Paul's, Harlington.

BLACKMAN Audrey Mary
Sister 318419 Queen Alexandra's Imperial Military Nursing Service, who died on Monday, 27th. November, 1944 aged 28.
She was the daughter of Albert and Alice Mary Blackman, of Hayes.
At the time Antwerp was still in range of V.1. s (pilotless ram-jet planes containing 1800 lbs. of explosives). She was killed as a result of one of these attacks. It is interesting to note that Nursing Sisters were treated as Officers and not non-commissioned officers.
She is buried at Schoonselhof Cemetery, Antwerp, Belgium. Grave 1. A. 35.

BLACKWELL Sidney Harold
Able Seaman P/JX 518474 H.M.S. *Manners*, Royal Navy, who died on Friday, 26th. January, 1945 aged 19.
He was the son of John and Elsie Grace Blackwell, of Hayes.
H.M.S. *Manners* was a *Captain* class frigate built in Boston, U.S.A. in 1943. She was torpedoed by U. 1172 with a homing torpedo in the Irish Sea, 21 miles west of Anglesey. Her stern was blown off, and she was towed to Barrow-in-Furness and laid up in a state of disrepair. U.1172 was hunted down and sunk five hours later. Thirty six men were lost, including Sidney, out of her complement of 200. He was buried at sea and is commemorated on the Portsmouth Naval Memorial. Panel 88 Column 3, and at St. Mary's, Hayes.

BLEASE Thomas Henry
Sergeant 348512 R.A.F. who died on Thursday, 9th. December, 1943.
He was the husband of Louisa H. Blease, of Hayes.
He was an aircraft chargehand on general duties with 210 Group. He died in his billet from a heart attack.
He is buried at El Alia Cemetery, Algeria. Grave 12. B. 16, and is commemorated at St. Mary's, Hayes. El Alia is13 kms. S. E. of Algiers

BOCKING Ronald John
Sergeant 1399616 R.A.F.V.R. who died on Wednesday, 19th. July, 1944 aged 20.
He was the son of Percy G. and Florence K. Bocking. of Hayes.
He was a navigator flying Lancaster 111 s with 100 Squadron of 1 Group based at Grimsby, Lincs.
They took off at 2303 hrs. to attack Scholven/Buer and crashed circa 0135 hrs. in the target area after
being crippled by flak. All seven of the crew, including Ronald were killed and rest in the
Reichswald Forest War Cemetery, Kleve, Nordrhein-Westfalen, Germany. Collective grave 20. A.
4-9. He is commemorated at St. Mary's Hayes, and St. Peter's and St. Paul's, Harlington.
160 aircraft attacked the oil plant and the raid was a complete success. Only four Lancasters were
lost.

BODIMEAD Ernest Arthur
Driver T/10687461 Royal Army Service Corps, who died on Friday, 23rd. April, 1943 aged 20.
He was the son of Sidney and May E. Bodimead, of Hayes.
The Allies had landed in North Africa on the 8th. November, 1942 (Operation *Torch*) and had
advanced to Tunisia. Ernest died in the Battle of the Medjez Plain which took place between the
23rd. and 30th of April. This was the penultimate battle in Tunisia and the Axis forces surrendered
on the 12th. May.
He is buried at Medjez-el-Bab War Cemetery, Tunisia. Grave 18. C. 11, and commemorated at St.
Mary's, Hayes.

BOWGETT Frank William
Lance Serjeant 6204064 1st. Battalion, Middlesex Regiment, who died on Friday, 9th. February,
1945 aged 26.
He was the son of Albert O. and Norah E. Bowgett, of Hayes.
The 1st. Battalion was part of the 51st. Highland Infantry Division, one of the most respected
divisions in the British Army. *Eisenhower* had decided to attack through the Reichwald as the
Siegfried Line did not extend so far north. The attack began on February 8th, when XXX British
Corps debouched from the constricted neck between the Mass and Rhine, south-east of Nijmegen.
XXX Corps consisted of five infantry divisions, supported by three armoured brigades and eleven
regiments of specialised armour. This attack (Operation *Veritable*) was launched after the most
concentrated artillery barrage of the war so far.
The Middx. armed with 72 Vickers Heavy machine guns fired over seven million rounds of
ammunition in this initial assault. Frank died on the second day and "after the most horrible
seventeen days of intense close quarter fighting in the forests, which were to be an infantry slogging
match" they cleared the Reichswald of the Germans. They could now prepare for the crossing of
the Rhine, and the advance into the Central Plain of Germany.
He is buried at the Reichswald Forest War Cemetery, Kleve, Nordrhein-Westfalen, Germany. Grave
56. E. 13, and commemorated at St. Mary's, Hayes.

BRADES Edward Victor
Able Seaman C/JX 162789 H.M.S. *Hermes*, Royal Navy, who died on Thursday, 9th. April, 1942
aged 18.
H.M.S. *Hermes* was a light fleet carrier of 10, 000 tons built in 1919. The Japanese fleet consisting
of three fast battleships, five Fleet carriers, and supporting cruisers and destroyers had sortied from
Singapore to attack shipping in the Indian Ocean near Ceylon. The British Eastern Fleet, being
outclassed, in preserving the theory of "the fleet in being" had made a made a strategic withdrawal to
the Maldives.

The *Hermes* was sunk by aircraft from the *Akagi, Hiryu,* (both later sunk at the battle of *Midway*) *Shokaku,* and *Zuikaku,* after being hit by over 40 * 500 lb. bombs. H.M.A.S. *Vampire,* an Australian destroyer was also sunk in this attack. 307 men were lost in the *Hermes* but the hospital ship *Vita* rescued over 600 survivors from both ships. Amazingly in what happened later in the war the status of the *Vita* as a hospital ship was respected by the Japanese, and not attacked.

Please note **Victor BREED** below who was the same age, enlisted at the same depot, and who died on the same ship. Note they are not commemorated on the same panel at Chatham.

He is commemorated on the Chatham Naval Memorial. Panel 53. 1, and St. Mary's, Hayes.

BREED Victor George
Ordinary Seaman C/JX 180509 H.M.S. *Hermes,* Royal Navy, who died on Thursday, 9th. April, 1942 aged 18.

He was the son of George H. and Georgina S. Breed, of Hayes.

He is commemorated on the Chatham Naval Memorial. Panel 57. 2, and St. Mary's, Hayes.

BRYAN Ronald Albert Edward
Trooper 2391139 2nd. Derbyshire Yeomanry, Royal Armoured Corps, who died on Wednesday, 18th. April, 1945 aged 21..

He was the son of Albert E. and Lily Bryan, of Hayes.

The 2nd. Derbyshire Yeomanry was the Reconnaissance Squadron of the 51st. Highland Infantry Division. Please see Frank **BOWGETT** who died in the fighting in the Reichswald. After the Reichswald they had successfully crossed the Rhine, and were now ready for the final advance into Germany.

Montgomery instructed by *Churchill* had orders to race to the Baltic, frustrate any advance by the Russians into Denmark, and prevent the Baltic becoming a Russian Sea.

XXX Corps including the Highlanders was directed on Bremen and Bremerhaven some 160 miles away via Enschede, Salzbegen, Lingen, Quakenbruk, Vechta, Wildeshausen and finally Delmenhorst. The Derbyshire Yeomanry led in their scout cars and light tanks reporting back, pushing, probing, and harrying the defenders. They began their advance on the 5th. April, and Ronald died in the capture of Delmenhorst which is just west of Bremen, on the 18th. There were just three weeks to go before the end of the fighting in Europe.

He is buried at Becklingen War Cemetery, Soltau, Niedersachsen, Germany. Grave 3. J. 12, and commemorated at St. Mary's Hayes.

BUCKLER Henry Charles Joseph
Sergeant 1600800 R.A.F.V.R. who died on Thursday, 3rd. August, 1944 aged 20.

He was the son of George H. and Dorothy G. Buckler, of Hayes.

He was a Wireless Operator / Air Gunner flying Lancaster 1 s with 166 Squadron of 1 Group based at Kirmington, Lincs. (just south of Hull). They took off at 1130 hrs. to attack the V 1 Flying Bomb sites at Trossy. Believed shot down by flak, just to the north of target area. Five of the crew died including Henry, but the Pilot was taken prisoner, and the Flight Engineer evaded capture.

He is buried at Creil Community Cemetery, Oise, France. Plot 1. Grave 393, and commemorated at St. Mary's, Hayes.

This was a successful operation, 114 aircraft despatched but seven Lancasters lost.

BUNCE Robert
Petty Officer C/J 101954 H.M.S. *Firedrake,* Royal Navy, who died on Thursday, 17th. December, 1942 aged 36.

He was the son of William and Elizabeth Bunce; husband of Dorcas Ellen May Bunce, of Hayes.

H.M.S. *Firedrake* was a destroyer of 1350 tons displacement built on the Tyne by Vickers. She was armed with 4 * 4.7 guns, 8 * 21 inch torpedo tubes and had a speed of 35 knots.
She was one of the escort of convoy ON 153. When 600 miles south of Iceland, out of range of friendly aircraft based there, at 2010 hrs. she was torpedoed by U. 211. She broke in half immediately. The bow portion sank quickly, leaving no survivors in that section. About thirty five of the crew clung to the stern portion and attracted the attention of H.M.S. *Sunflower* by firing starshells. However the stern sank as *Sunflower* approached and she was able to rescue only twenty six men in the very heavy seas. So one hundred and seventy one crew were therefore lost including Robert.
He is commemorated on the Chatham Naval Memorial. Panel 51. 3, and also at St. Mary's, Hayes, and St. Peter's, and St. Paul's, Harlington.

BURRELL Derek Thomas
Flight Sergeant 1865843 R.A.F.V.R. who died on Tuesday, 16th. October, 1945 aged 20.
He was the son of Charles D. and Rosa E. Burrell, of Hayes.
He was a Wireless Operator / Air Gunner serving with the Mediterranean and Middle East Communication Squadron based at Marcianise, Italy.(near Naples) He died when his Wellington X crashed at 1433 hrs. at Capodichino airfield.
He is buried at Naples War Cemetery, Italy. Grave 1V. M. 14, and commemorated at St. Mary's, Hayes.

BURTON James
Able Seaman P/JX 604014 H.M.S. *Isis*, Royal Navy who died on Thursday, 20th. July, 1944 aged 19.
He was the son of Samuel and Elizabeth Burton, of Hayes.
H.M.S. *Isis* was an I Class destroyer originally intended for Turkey. She was sunk 6 miles north of Arromanches, Normandy, but her loss was not known until 0209 hrs, on the 21st. when H.M.S. *Hound* rescued 20 survivors. But eleven officers, and 143 ratings, including James had been killed. It was originally thought that she was sunk by either a mine or a torpedo from a U Boat. But just in the last few years, after extensive underwater research it has been discovered that she was sunk by an Hs 293 Glider Bomb launched by Dornier bomber. This was a radio controlled bomb guided by the bomb-aimer visually from the aircraft. There is a very good documentary about this which is shown on one of the History Channels from time to time. John Warrick of Ruislip died in the sloop *Egret* on the 27th. August, 1943, his ship being the first ever casualty of the same type of guided missile.
He is commemorated on the Portsmouth Naval Memorial. Panel 82. Column 1, and at St. Mary's. Hayes.

BURTON Robert Henry
Guardsman 2617587 1st. Battalion, Grenadier Guards, who died on Saturday, 23rd. September, 1944 aged 27.
He was the son of Harry and Lily Burton,; husband of Doris Burton, of Hayes.
The 1st. Battalion was part of the Guards Armoured Division, armed with Sherman tanks, who as part of XXX Corps were desperately trying to reach Arnhem to link up with the 1st. Airborne. He died in the final attempts before the evacuation on the night of 24/25th. September.
He is buried at Uden War Cemetery, Noord-Brabant, Holland. Grave 3. 1. 6.
Please see note after Alexander **BAISDEN**

CAMPBELL William Robert
Sergeant 1853822 R.A.F.V.R. who died on Wednesday, 30th. August, 1944.
He was an Air Gunner flying Lancaster 1 s with 50 Squadron of 5 Group based at Skellingthorpe Lincs. They took off at 2059 hrs. to attack Konigsberg, in the Baltic.
All the crew of seven died and are buried at Helsingborg (Palsjo) Municipal Cemetery, Sweden Collective Grave Sec. XV 76-80. This is the same cemetery that Sergeants Donald P. Aplin and Edward C. Slaughter (see above) who died on the 8th. February, 1945 are buried .
189 Lancasters were sent to attack this target at the limit of their extreme range. This attack was very successful. Bomber Command estimated that 41 % of the housing and 20 per cent of the all the industry in Konigsberg was destroyed. There was heavy fighter opposition (who probably damaged William's aircraft causing it to crash in Sweden), and 15 Lancasters were lost.
William is commemorated at St. Mary's, Hayes.

CANFIELD Edward James
Leading Telegraphist C/J 74086 Royal Navy, H.M.S. *Samphire*, who died on Saturday, 30th. January, 1943 aged 42.
The *Samphire* was a *Flower* class corvette of 1015 tons displacement completed in 1941. She was an anti-submarine vessel based on the design of a whaler, with a speed of 16 knots.
She was in the Western Mediterranean, 30 miles north-east of Bougie when she was sunk by a Axis submarine. There is some doubt which submarine torpedoed her. Both the U. 596 and the Italian submarine *Platini* claimed to have sunk her. She went down very quickly and unfortunately only 4 survivors were picked up by H.M.S. *Zetland*, 81 being lost including Edward.
He is commemorated on the Chatham Naval Memorial Panel 71.1, and St. Mary's, Hayes.

CARBUTT Clifford
Private 5345965 7th. Battalion, Oxford and Bucks Light Infantry, who died on Wednesday, 29th. September, 1943.
He was the son of Arthur and Eva Carbutt, husband of Florence Ada Carbutt, of Edmonton.
The 7th. Ox. and Bucks was part of the 1st. London Infantry Brigade of the 56th. London Infantry Division. and they landed at Salerno on the 9th. September, 1943. The beaches at Salerno are perfectly formed for a landing operation, twenty miles in length and within fighter range (250 miles) of Sicily. The object of Operation Avalanche was to seize Naples, and use it as the port to supply the Allied troops in Italy. A few hours after the landings the Italians announced they were at peace with the Allies. The Germans who had been expecting this and started to move their troops south to stop the allies advancing inland. Clifford survived the heavy fighting at Salerno but died in the battle for the capture of Naples which fell on the 1st. October.
He is buried at Salerno War Cemetery, Italy Grave 111 B 25, and commemorated at St. Mary's, Hayes. It is said that the Italians never end a war on the same side as they entered, but that is not correct. In the first world war they were neutral, and they entered it on the side of the Allies only after being promised Trieste and the Dalmation coast when victory was achieved.

CAREY Francis Henry   DSM
Able Seaman C/J 73214 H.M.S. *Firedrake* Royal Navy, who died on Thursday, 17th,. December, 1942 aged 41.
He was the husband of Mrs. L. E. Carey, of Hayes.
Please see Robert **BUNCE** for details of the *Firedrake's* sinking.
He is commemorated on the Chatham Naval Memorial, Panel 53.2. and at St. Mary's, Hayes.
The London Gazette of 8th. September, 1942 stated that he was awarded the Distinguished Service Medal for devotion to duty.

CARPENTER Reginald William
Sergeant 1382644 R.A.F.V.R. who died on Thursday, 6th. January, 1944
He was a Wireless/Operator Air Gunner flying Lancaster 1 s with 619 Squadron of 5 Group from Woodhall Spa, Lincs.
They took off at 0018 hrs. to attack Stettin Germany, (now Szczecin, Poland) and crashed in the target area.
The crew of seven are all buried at Poznan Old Garrison Cemetery. Poland. Reginald's grave is 6. A. 9. Poznan is in north-western Poland, to the east of Szczecin. He is commemorated at St. Mary's, Hayes.
348 Lancasters and 10 Halifaxes took part in this raid, the first on this target since September 1941. The Mosquito diversion to Berlin kept most of the German fighters away from the main force but Ronald's was one of the 16 aircraft lost. The raid started accurately but the bombing drifted away to the west. Heavy damage was done, 244 people were killed and over a 1,000 injured.

CARTER John Thomas
Staff Sergeant 6458816 Royal Electrical and Mechanical Engineers, who died on Saturday, 11th. March, 1944 aged 26.
He was the son of John J. and Dorothy Carter; husband of Mary Carter, of Hayes.
He died at the General Hospital, Margate of " peritonitis due to extension of inflammation from wounds in the groin and abdomen, and the effects of blast on the intestines due to the explosion of a fused bag of ammonal which he was about to throw in the course of a Military tactical exercise on the 2nd. March."
He is buried at Hayes and Harlington (Cherry Lane) Cemetery. Sec. R. 1. Grave N. 2. He is commemorated at St. Mary's, Hayes.

CARTER Leonard Joe
Corporal T/151708 Royal Army Service Corps, who died on Monday, 13th. December, 1943 aged 33.
He was the son of William J. and Florence M. Carter, of Hayes.
He died of natural causes at Wimborne Avenue, Hayes. In civilian life he was a postman.
He is buried at Hayes and Harlington (Cherry Lane) Cemetery. Sec. C. 2. Grave G. 31

CARTER Leslie George
Gunner 1164223 5 Regiment, Royal Horse Artillery, who died on Tuesday, 15th. December, 1942 aged 31.
He was the son of Mr. and Mrs. George Carter; husband of Beatrix Rosa Carter, of Hayes.
The Axis forces were now in full retreat after their defeat at El Alamein, but the pursuit by 8th. Army was slow and cautious. As *Rommel's* next tenable defensive position would clearly be at El Agheila, west of the Cyrenaican bulge, an attempt was made to cut him off - to re-enact the success of General O'Connor in February, 1941.
The battle of El Agheila took place between the 14-17th. of December and Leslie died on the second day. *Rommel* was able to slip away, but Cyrenaica was now free of Axis troops, and the Allies could use the ports of Tobruk and Benghazi.
He is commemorated on the Alamein Memorial, Egypt. Column 6.

CHURCH Charles Edward
Sergeant 1425432 R.A.F.V.R. who died on Friday, 4th. August, 1944 aged 24.
He was the son of Mr. and Mrs. C. W.. Church, of Hayes.

He was a Flight Engineer flying Dakota 111 s with 353 Squadron based at Palam, near New Delhi. He was a passenger on a Dakota returning from Calcutta on a routine mail run when it crashed in a heavy storm near Mohania, 11 miles north east of their base. The crew of three in the Dakota were also killed.

He is buried at Ranchi War Cemetery, India, Grave 5. E. 2, and commemorated at St. Mary's, Hayes, and St. Peter's and St. Paul's, Harlington. Ranchi is in the state of Bihar, 400 kms. north-west of Calcutta.

CLARE Thomas
Fusilier 7016190 2nd. Battalion, Royal Inniskilling Fusiliers, who died on Thursday, 13th. April, 1944 aged 24.

He was the son of Harry and Alice Clare, of Hayes.

Please see note below.

The 3rd. "Skins" was part of the 13th. Infantry Brigade of the 5th. Infantry Division which had left the U.K. to take part in the invasion of Sicily in July, 1943. They then took part in the crossings of the rivers Sangro and Garisilano in Italy and were sent to Anzio as reinforcements. Thomas was killed in the comparatively quiet days before the break-out in late May.

He is buried at Beach Head War Cemetery, Anzio, Italy. Grave X111. A. 3, and commemorated at St. Mary's, Hayes.

ANZIO

To outflank the *Gustav* Line based on Cassino and just north of Naples it was decided to land at Anzio, just south of Rome, (Operation *Shingle*). This took place on the 22nd. January, 3rd. U.S. Infantry on the right, and 1st. British Infantry on the left. The landing was unopposed and they advanced 7 miles inland with a front of twenty-six. It was supposed to link up with the advance from Cassino sixty miles to the south, but this attempt on the *Gustav* Line failed. Two divisions were not strong enough (eight landed at Normandy) but the Navy said they could not support any more. As Winston Churchill said:-

"I thought we were throwing a wildcat onto the beach to rip the bowels out of the Boche. Instead we have landed a whale"

The Germans treated the landing as the Invasion of Europe and rushed troops there. By the 28th. January 4 divisions were in place and by the 5th. February, five, including one Panzer division. The Allies dug in and were reinforced by two U.S. Divisions, the 35th. and the 1st. Armoured on the 12th. February and the 56th. British Infantry Division was also sent there. Heavy fighting took place throughout February but by the 29th. the Germans were exhausted and never threatened again. Probably it was the Allied airforces who repeatedly bombed and straffed the German positions that were the decisive factor.

The Germans had brought forward two huge 240 mm. railway guns called "Leopold" and "Robert" which kept the beach under constant fire. To avoid these barrages the Allied troops learned to walk in a special Anzio crouch to avoid the German artillery spotters.

The *Gustav* Line was finally broken at Monte Cassino on the 25th. May and the link up from the south took place on the 30th. May. Rome fell on the 5th. June, 1944.

The following also died in the fighting at Anzio.

A.E. Cripps Royal Berkshire Regiment 12.3.44,

F.W.Day Northamptonshie Regiment 7.2.44,

W.G. Haynes :Lincolnshire Regiment 4.2.44

F.A. Otter Grenadier Guards 17.1.44,

A.H.Prior Royal Artillery 17.2.44

CLARK Alan Gerald
Aircraftman 2nd. Class 1814448 R.A.F.V.R. who died on Monday, 24th. July, 1944 aged 17.
He was training as a Flight Engineer with No.3. (Pilots) Advanced Flying Unit based at South
Cerney, Glos. He died when his Oxford trainer crashed on the Powick-Malvern Road, Worcs. The
Oxford was a twin engined plane used to train bomber and transport crews.
He is buried at Hayes and Harlington (Cherry Lane) Cemetery. Sec. G. 1. Grave O.2, and
commemorated at St. Mary's, Hayes.

CLARKE S
Although commemorated at St. Mary's, Hayes, unfortunately I have not been able to trace this
person

COASTER Kenneth William
Leading Aircraftman 1803392 R.A.F.V.R. who died on Friday, 17th. September, 1943 aged 19.
He was the son of Alfred and Ethel Coaster, of Hayes.
He was under training as a pilot with No.1 British Flying Training School at Terrell, Texas. (just east
of Dallas). He was flying a Harvard trainer when he was involved in an accident and crashed at
Wrxahachee? Texas.
He is buried at Terrell (Oakland) Memorial Park, Texas, U.S.A. R.A.F. Plot. Grave 16, and
commemorated at St. Mary's Hayes.

COLLINS Reginald William
Marine CH/X 1062 H.M.S. *Arethusa*, Royal Marines, who died on Wednesday, 18th. November,
1942 aged 26.
He was the son of Florence Annie Collins, of Hayes.
H.M.S. *Arethusa* was a light cruiser of the *Arethusa* class, of 5,000 tons, built in 1933 with six inch
guns. She was escorting a Malta convoy when she was hit on the forward turrets by an aerial
torpedo launched by a German aircraft. 159 men were killed including Reginald and most of the
Marine detachment. She was towed back to Alexandria by *H.M.S. Petard.* This took three days so
badly had she been damaged. It was usually the task of the Marines to man the large guns on a ship.
He is commemorated on the Chatham Naval Memorial. Panel 65. 2. and St. Matthew's, Yiewsley.

COLLINS Ronald Frank
Engine Room Artificer 4th. Class C/MX 119444 H.M.S. *Goodall* Royal Navy, who died on Sunday,
29th. April, 1945 aged 25.
He was the son of William F. and Edith J. Collins, of Hayes.
H.M.S. *Goodall* was a Captain class frigate of 1085 tons, built in 1943 and named after Capt.
Samuel *Goodall.* of H.M.S. *Defiance.* She was the last British warship to be sunk by a submarine in
WW2. The frigate was engaged in an anti-U. boat sweep to clear the waters of the Kola Inlet in the
Artic of submarines before the departure of convoy RA 66 to the U.K. After the torpedo from U.
968 hit, her magazine exploded and blew away the forward part of the ship. She was beyond
salvage so was abandoned and scuttled. Ninety-eight of the crew were killed including Ronald.
He is commemorated on the Chatham Naval Memorial. Panel 81.2. and at St. Mary's Hayes.

COLTON Thomas Christopher
Guardsman 6096248 2nd. Battalion, Irish Guards, who died on Tuesday, 1st. August, 1944 aged 24.
He was the son of Thomas and Sarah Colton, of Hayes.
The 2nd. Battalion were part of the 5th.Armoured Brigade of the Guards Armoured Division. They
had Sherman tanks and arrived in Normandy on the June 27th. 1944 (D-Day + 21). They had fought

hard in Normandy and were now taking part in a six division attack near Mount Pincon, to prevent German troops being transferred to the American flank as *Bradley* had broken through at St. Lo and was advancing southwards. Into battle roared *"St. Patrick"*, *"Ulster"*, *"Leinster"*, and *"Connaught"*, *"Achill"*, *"Bantry"*, *"Cloneen"*, and sixty-seven other tanks with Irish place-names. But unfortunately Thomas killed in this advance. The Shermans had a dreadful record of catching fire when hit and were nicknamed "Ronsons" after the cigarette lighter because of this.

He is commemorated on the Bayeux Memorial, Calvados, France. Panel 12, Column 2, and at St. Mary's, Hayes.

CONNELL Horace Arthur

Trooper 7906099 3rd. County of London Yeomanry (Sharpshooters), Royal Armoured Corps, who died on Wednesday, 2nd. September, 1942 aged 25.

He was the husband of Doris Mary Connell, of Harlington.

The 3rd. County of London Yeomanry, armed with American *Grant* tanks, was part of the 22nd. Armoured Brigade, of the 7th. Armoured Division (The Desert Rats). The Axis had advanced to El Alamein on the Egyptian border and in August *Churchill* and *Alanbrooke* decided to replace *Auckinleck* with *Montgomery*.

There now took place the Battle of *Alam Halfa* (also known at the 1st. Battle of *El Alamein*). *Rommel*'s plan was his usual tactic of breaking through in the south and carrying out a right hook to the coast, where the only reliable road from Libya to Egypt ran. *Montgomery*'s tactics were to defeat *Rommel* but preserve his tanks for the later vital battle. This he did, *Rommel* was forced to go on the defensive, and *Montgomery* lost only 67 out of 700 tanks. The battle took place between the 30th. August and the 2nd. September, and Horace died on the final day. On the 4th November after being hugely reinforced *Montgomery* won the 2nd. Battle of El Alamein, and the Axis was in full retreat.

He is buried at El. Alamein War Cemetery, Egypt. Grave X11. E.7. He is commemorated at St. Mary's. Harmondsworth

COOKE Cyril Stephen

Petty Officer Wireman P/MX 89128 H.M.S. *Janus*, Royal Navy, who died on Sunday, 23rd. January, 1944 aged 32.

He was the son of Thomas and Emily C. Cooke; husband of Winifred Margaret Cooke, of Hayes.

H.M.S. *Janus* was a destroyer of 1690 tons built in 1930. She was armed with 6 * 4.7 inch guns, 10 * 21 inch torpedo tubes, a speed of 35 knots, and a complement of 183. She was attacked off Anzio Beach, Rome, at dusk by a German dive bomber, using both conventional torpedoes and wireless controlled glider bombs. A torpedo set off her magazine and she sank in twenty-two minutes with the loss of 162 sailors including Cyril.

He is commemorated on the Portsmouth Naval Memorial. Panel 86. Column 3.

COOPER Dennis Lionel

Flight Sergeant 1331029 R.A.F.V.R. who died on Thursday, 25th. November, 1943 aged 21.

He was the son of Percival and Katherine Cooper; husband of Mrs. P.S. Cooper, of Harlington.

He was an Air Gunner flying Wellington X s with 40 Squadron based at Oudna 1, south of Tunis. He was taking part in a bombing raid on Turin, Italy, when his aircraft was shot down somewhere over the sea near Sardinia.

This was the same squadron Royston **WORKMAN**, of Hayes was with when he was killed in November, 1942

He is commemorated on the Malta Memorial. Panel 7 Column 1.

21

COOPER Kenneth Ernest
Private 7626126 Royal Army Ordnance Corps, attached 1st. Indian Infantry Brigade, who died on Friday, 5th. December, 1941 aged 25.
He was the son of Ernest and Laura Cooper; husband of Elsie Mabel Cooper, of Hayes.
The Eighth Army had launched Operation *Crusader* to reconquer Cyrenania and relieve the siege of Tobruk. They crossed the border and after seven weeks of hard fighting had achieved their objectives, but unfortunately Kenneth died in the final attack.
On the 6th. December Rommel decided he could no longer hold on at Tobruk, The German forces still on the Egyptian border had to be abandoned and were taken into captivity. Behind a vigorous show of strength, to inhibit too attentive a pursuit (in which Kenneth was killed) Rommel slipped away. He now retreated to Gazala and there he waited for reinforcements to continue his advance in 1942 but which resulted in his defeat at El Alamein in October.
He is commemorated on the Alamein Memorial. Column 84

COSSOM Ernest Edward Alan
Private 5383976 9th. Battalion, Durham Light Infantry, who died on Wednesday, 7th. June, 1944 aged 31.
He was the son of Alan and Emily E. Cossom; husband of Maud Cossom, of Hayes.
The 9th. Battalion was part of the 151st. Infantry Brigade of the 50th. (Northumberland) Infantry Division who landed on the 6th. June, 1944 on Gold Beach, which was on the right flank of the British and Canadian forces. They advanced quickly inland and on the 7th. had taken Bayeaux and were digging in on the high ground to the south and south-east of the city, and the Bayeaux-Caen highway was also in Allied hands. Ernest died in the heavy fighting to enable these objects to be achieved.
He is buried at Bayeaux War Cemetery, Calvados. Grave X1V. J. 7, and commemorated at St. Mary's, Hayes.

COULTRUP Thomas
Civilian, Light Rescue Service, who died on Friday, 18th. December 1942 aged 42.
He was the husband of Annie L. Coultrup of 12, Ashford Avenue, Hayes.
He was injured on the 14th. December, at Uxbridge Road, and died at Hillingdon County Hospital. Uxbridge. He is commemorated at St. Mary's, Hayes.

COWLEY Joseph William
Corporal 6478438 1st. Battalion, Royal Fusiliers (City of London Regiment), who died on Sunday, 5th. December, 1943 aged 32.
He was the son of William and Emily Cowley; husband of Priscilla Cowley, of Hayes.
The 1st. Battalion together with the 1/12 Frontier Force Regiment and 1/6th. Royal Gurkha Rifles formed the 17th. Indian Brigade of the 8th. Indian Infantry Division. They had arrived in Italy to join 8th. Army in September from Egypt. They then advanced northwards with their flank on the Adriatic coast. The Germans were masters of defensive tactics, and using the terrain wisely made any advance costly and difficult. The Brigade had just taken part in the battle to cross the river Sangro, which was three hundred yards wide, five foot deep, turbulent and flooded, and had proved a serious obstacle.
The Eighth Army had now succeeded in establishing a sound beachhead on the north bank. Joseph died in the patrolling which took place before they advanced northwards and captured the town of Caldari.
He is buried at the Sangro River War Cemetery, Italy. Grave X1. D. 22.

COX Charles Herbert
Gunner 840607 8 Heavy Anti-Aircraft Regiment, Royal Artillery, who died on Tuesday, 2nd. June, 1942 aged 24.
He was the son of Charles H. and Clara M. Cox, of Hayes.
The 8th. Regiment was stationed at Peshawar, India and was sent to Burma in May 1942 to help resist the Japanese invasion. They then took part in the fierce fighting and the "Long Retreat" back to India and the regiment reached Dalhousie on the 22nd. of June. But Charles had been wounded, was sent back earlier, and died in one of the hospitals in Bihar.
He is buried at Ranchi War Cemetery, India. Grave 8. M. 6.

CRIPPS Albert Edward
Private 5345677 10th. Battalion, Royal Berkshire Regiment, who died on Monday, 7th. February, 1944 aged 30.
He was the son of Edward T. and Alice Cripps; husband of Lilian Cripps, of Harlington.
Please see note after Thomas **CLARE**
The 10th. Battalion was part of the 2nd. London Infantry Brigade of the 56th. London Infantry Division, which was transferred to the 1st. Infantry Division on the 3rd. February, 1944. Albert died when the Germans, now with five divisions, launched their major attacks to drive the Allies into the sea.
He is buried at Beach Head War Cemetery, Anzio, Italy. Grave XX1. C. 5. He is commemorated at St. Mary's, Harmondsworth.

CRONIN Robert
Serjeant 3382900 1st. Battalion, East Lancashire Regiment, who died on Sunday, 7th. January, 1945 aged 35.
He was the son of John. H. and Elizabeth A. Cronin, of Hayes.
The 1st. Battalion was part of the 158 Brigade of the 43rd. Welsh Infantry Division, who had landed in Normandy and fought their way across France and Belgium to Holland.
On the 16th December, 1944 the Wehrmacht launched their final offensive in the West. 5th and 6th. Panzer Armies attacked the weakly held sector in the Ardennes. The Battle of the Ardennes was an American battle and an American victory. But to safeguard Antwerp British forces were sent to hold the line at the river Meuse as "long stop" in case the Germans broke through. Hotton was the on the western limit of the German advance and Robert died here on the 7th. On the 8th. *Hitler* gave the order to withdraw and the battle was over.
He is buried at Hotton War Cemetery, Hotton, Luxembourg. Grave 1V.B. 8, and commemorated at St. Mary's, Hayes.

CRUTCHFIELD Peter Neller
Sergeant 1324786 R.A.F.V.R. who died on Friday, 12th. May, 1944 aged 20.
He was the son of Aruther and Edith Crutchfield, of Hayes.
He was a Wireless Operator / Air gunner flying Lancaster 111 s with 103 Squadron of 1 Group based at Elsham Wolds, Lincs. They took of at 2158 hrs. to bomb the railway yards at Hasselt, Belgium. They were shot down by a night-fighter of 1.NJC1 Squadron and crashed 0200 hrs. at Loenhout, some 24 kms. north east of Antwerp. 131 aircraft were despatched, the target well marked, 39 aircraft bombed, but all missed the target because of thick haze, The Master Bomber ordered the bombing to stop, and all aircraft to return home, but 5 Lancasters including Peter's were lost.
The crew are buried in the joint grave 1Va. E. 50 at Schoonselhof Cemetery, Antwerp. He is commemorated at St. Mary's. Hayes.

CURNOW Frederick Walter
Gunner 1140682 138 Field Regiment, Royal Artillery, who died on Tuesday, 17th. November, 1942 aged 19.
He was the son of Edwin W. and Ethel E. Curnow, of Hayes.
The 138 Field Regiment was part of the 78th. Infantry (Battleaxe) Division of the British 1st. Army which landed in North Africa (*Operation Torch*) on the 8th. November, 1942. They were on the left flank with the object of capturing Algiers and advancing into Tunisia.
Leaving the Americans to deal with the Vichy French and take control of Algiers, the 78th. moved eastwards on the 11th. When the Allies had landed Tunisia had been free of German troops but *Kesselring* soon rushed in troops by sea and air.
The 138 armed with 25 pounder field guns was helping the Royal West Kents hold Djebel Aboud when the first counter-attack from the Germans was made, and Frederick died on the first day of the battle. After holding out for eight days the Royal West Kents were relieved by the Argyll and Sutherland Highlanders.
He is buried at Tabarka Ras Rajel War Cemetery, Tunisia. Grave 4. D. 1. Tabarka is a coastal town on the Tunisian/Algerian borders. He is commemorated at St. Mary's, Hayes.

CURRIE Frank
Serjeant 2045034 87 Light Anti-Aircraft Regiment, Royal Artillery, who died on Monday, 17th. April, 1944 aged 35.
He was the son of Samuel B. and Eliza Currie; husband of Mabel Currie, of Feamington Place Hayes.
He died at the Royal Naval Hospital, Portland, from shock and multiple injuries sustained when a hand grenade exploded when he was checking ammunition at Portland.
He is buried at Portland Royal Naval Cemetery, Dorset. Grave 736.

CURTIS Stephen
Driver T/2050563 718 (Airborne) Light Component Company, Royal Army Service Corps, who died on Saturday, 10th. June, 1944 aged 24.
He was the son of Stephen and Beatrice E. Curtis, of ,Hayes.
The 718 Light Component Company was part of the 5th. Parachute Brigade, 6th. Airborne Division, whose aim was to secure the left flank of the Normandy invasion beaches. On the 6th June, 1944 five minutes after midnight six gliders carrying the Ox. & Bucks. troops landed on top of the two bridges over the *Orne* river and canal to the east of Caen and seized them.
Whilst the glider-borne force securing the bridges, the pathfinders who had parachuted down near Ranville were hastening to mark out the dropping zone for the 2,200 men of the 5th. Parachute Brigade (including Stephen) who were due in at 12.50 a.m. Although the drop was not entirely successful due to the winds, they had secured the dropping zone for the 72 gliders which were bringing in the main force. They then secured the right flank of their dropping zone and linked up with the British seaborne troops in the morning.
The Germans counter-attacked repeatedly but the paratroopers held their ground. Stephen was killed during one of these attacks on the fourth day.
General R. Gale the commander of the division said, quoting Shakespeare's Henry V
"And gentleman in England now abed,
Should think themselves accursed that they were not here"
He is buried at Ranville War Cemetery, Calvados, France. Grave 1A. J. 14, and commemorated at St. Mary's. Hayes

CUST Philip Gordon
Sergeant 1388747 R.A.F.V.R. who died on Monday, 8th, February, 1943 aged 32.
He was the son of Gladys Annie Cust, of Hayes.
He was a trainee Bomb Aimer with 10 Operational Training Unit, Bomber Command, based at
Abingdon, Oxon. They took off at 0056 hrs. in a Whitley V (a twin engined Bomber, in 1943
virtually obsolete for front line service) on a night exercise, during which they attempted to land at
Harwell. Berks. On touchdown, the Whitley bounced badly and while going round again crashed at
0116 hrs a mile or so SSW of the airfield. Four of the crew were killed, including Philip, but one of
them survived.
He is buried at Brookwood Military Cemetery, Surrey. Grave 22. B.12.

DANIELS Gwilym
Leading Aircraftman 1384200 R.A.F.V.R, who died on Tuesday, 15th. January, 1946 aged 34.
He was the son of Daniel and Mary A. Daniels, of Hayes End.
He was a Fitter 11 with 271 Squadron flying Dakota transports from Broadwell, Oxon., (near Brize
Norton). He was a passenger on a Dakota whose route was Bordeaux, Aden, Bahrain, and Lydda,
and when en route from Bordeaux to Aden crashed at Callalonbue, 5 miles south of Marseilles. when
it flew into a hillside.
He is buried at Mazarques War Cemetery, Marseilles, Bouches-du-Rhone, France. Plot 10. Row A.
Grave 22.

DAVIS Ernest John Walter
Flight Sergeant 1254697 R.A.F.V.R. who died on Thursday, 18th. February, 1943 aged 24.
He was the son of Mr. and Mrs. E. J. Davis; husband of Eileen Rachel Davis, of Hayes.
He was a pilot flying Lancaster 111 s with 9 Squadron of 5 Group based at Waddington, Lincs.
They took to bomb Wilhelmshaven, but crashed in the vicinity of Jever. Four of the crew died
including Ernest and they are buried at Sage War Cemetery, Oldenburg, Niedersachsen. Ernest's is
Grave 8. B. 3. The other three were taken prisoner, but to save his life Sgt. Fullard, the Flight
Engineer had to have his right leg amputated.
195 aircraft were despatched, 4 Lancasters lost, bombing was not very accurate but damage to
several buildings, including "Heine's Hotel (I do not know why this is highlighted, any ideas ?)

DAY Frank William
Warrant Officer Class 11, 5582265 Company Sergeant Major 2nd. Battalion, Northamptonshire
Regiment, who died on Sunday, 19th. March, 1944 aged 33.
He was the son of Ethel M. Day; husband of Sarah Ann Day, of Hayes.
Please see note after Thomas **CLARE.**
The 2nd. Battalion was part of the 17th. Brigade of the 5th. Infantry Division. On the 3rd. February,
the Germans, now with five divisions, launched their major counter-attacks to drive the Allies into
the sea, and Frank was killed in the heavy fighting defending the beachhead..
He is buried at Beach Head War Cemetery, Anzio, Rome. Grave V111. C. 3, and commemorated at
St. Mary's, Hayes.

DAY Peter
Sergeant 2213761 R.A.F.V.R. who died on Sunday 7th. January, 1945.
He lived at Fairholme Crescent, Hayes
He was an Air Gunner flying Lancaster 111 s with 170 Squadron of 1 Group based at Hemswell,
Lincs. .They took off at 1826 hrs. to attack Munich and were shot down over the target.

365 Lancasters and 9 Mosquitoes were despatched on this successful raid, from which 15 aircraft failed to return.

All seven of the crew were killed and are buried at Durnbach War Cemetery. Bad Tolz, Bayern, Germany. Collective grave 4. H. 27-30. Durnbach is a village 16 kms. east of Bad Tolz, a town 48 kms. south of Munich. He is commemorated at Bishopshalt School where he was a former pupil. It was Harold MacMillan who said that "Bomber Command was the Grammar Schoolboy's Somme".

DAYKIN David
Company Quartermaster Serjeant 4606406 1st. Battalion, Duke of Wellington's (West Riding Regiment), who died on Sunday, 7th. November. 1943 aged 41.

He was the son of Edward J. and Margaret Daykin,; husband of Maria Daykin, of Hayes.

The 1st. Battalion was part of the 3rd. Infantry Brigade of the 1st. Infantry Division who had been in North Africa since March 1943 and were due to go to Italy on the 7th. December. They had spent two months in the summer occupying the island of Pantelleria.

He died as a result of a traffic accident.

He is buried at Medjez-el-Bab War Cemetery, Tunisia. Grave 13. A. 15.

DEAMER Charles
Air Raid Warden who died on Wednesday, 19th. February, 1944 aged 47.

He lived at 10, Drenon Square, Hayes and was killed at Longmead Road, Hayes. He is commemorated at St. Mary's Hayes.

The bombs that fell on Longmead Road also killed the following;

MICKLEWRIGHT Frederick Henry, of 58 Drenon Square.

TIMMS Henry, Fireguard, 10. Drenon Square, Hayes.

WILLIAMS Edward George, aged 14, son of Mr. and Mrs. Edward Williams of 29. Longmead Road.

KELLY Columb, aged 30, of 31, Longmead Road from Offaly, Irish Republic.

KELLY Kathleen Sarah Alice, aged 21, his wife, of Hayes

KELLY Joseph aged 3, their son

PIKE Maria aged 79, of 37, Longmead Road.

PIKE Reginald aged 44, son of Maria.

BACON Ivy Ellen, daughter of Mrs. and the late Edward Bacon was injured by the same bomb at St. Mary's Walk and died at Hillingdon County Hospital, on the 25th. February.

Frederick H. Micklewright, Henry Timms are also commemorated at St. Mary's, Hayes.

On the 5th. September 1940 William and his wife, Mabel Deamer were killed at School House. Phelps Way, Harlington. I would think they must have been related to Charles

DEAN George Anthony
Corporal 10535678 1st. Battalion, East Yorkshire Regiment, who died on Friday, 1st. December, 1944 aged 32.

He was the son of Ernest and Lucy A. Dean; husband of Catherine Dean, of Hayes.

The 1st. Battalion was part of the 150th. Indian Infantry Brigade, training in India and waiting to go into action in Burma in the New Year. During this training George was killed in a traffic accident.

He is buried at Madras War Cemetery, Chenna, India. Grave 1.K. 8, and commemorated at St. Mary's, Hayes, and St. Peter's and St. Paul's, Harlington.

DEANE Cyril
Gunner 11000078 524 Coast Regiment, Royal Artillery who died on Saturday, 20th. June, 1942 aged 21.
He was the son of Alfred and Emma Deane, of Botwell Common Road, Hayes.
He died at Hillingdon Hospital, Uxbridge of a pulmonary embolism during an operation. In civilian life he was a general labourer.
He is buried at Hayes and Harlington (Cherry Lane) Cemetery. Sec G.1. Grave J.11.

DENNIS Archibald James
Lance Corporal 1883566 271 Field Company, Royal Engineers, who died on Monday, 2nd. April, 1945 aged 30.
He was the son of Walter H. and Louie Dennis; husband of Lily Dennis, of Hayes.
271 Field Company was part of the divisional troops of the 46th. Infantry Division fighting in Italy. On the 14th. January 1945 they were sent to Greece, where a civil war was going on between the Communist Resistance ELAS and the right wing monarchists. Dennis was killed in action but he was very unfortunate because the division left Greece five days later on the 7th. April.
He is buried at Phaleron War Cemetery, Athens. Grave 15. A. 1.

DENNIS Robert Edward Arthur
Driver T/124067 Royal Army Service Corps, who died on Sunday, 22nd. June, 1941 aged 23.
He was the son of John and Rose Dennis, of Hayes.
He died in an accident at Tingwall in the Orkney Isles. Tingwall is 15kms. north of the naval base at Scapa Flow.
He is buried at Hayes and Harlington (Cherry Lane) Cemetery, Sec. C. 1. Grave O. 31, commemorated at St. Mary's Hayes, and at St. Peter's and St. Paul's, Harlington.

DEVANEY John Irving
Private 13047205 Pioneer Corps, who died on Wednesday, 26th. February, 1941 aged 25.
He was the son of Edward and Ann Devaney of 131, Boston Street, Wigton Road, Carlisle; husband of Hilda Irene Devaney, of Hayes.
He was injured in an air raid and died at the Isolation Hospital, Roman Road, East Ham South, London.
He is buried at Carlisle (Dalston Road) Cemetery, Cumbria. Ward 11. Sec. P. Grave 9.

DEVENNEY Michael Raymond
Private 14408223 The Hallamshire Battalion, York and Lancaster Regiment, who died on Sunday, 25th. June, 1944 aged 18.
He was the son of Patrick and Hannah Devenney, of Bolton, Lancs.
The Hallamshire Battalion was part of the 146th. Infantry Brigade of the 49th. West Riding Infantry Division, (known as the Polar Bears because of the emblem on their vehicles). They had landed in Normandy on the 12th. June, (D-Day +6).
Michael died in the Battle of the Odon river which took place between the 25th. June and the 2nd. July. The Allies launched their attack to the west of Caen in one of their many attempts to break out of Normandy. Although it was not successful it succeeded in making the Germans move more of their armour to face the British and Canadians. and leave the Americans on the right flank with less opposition, which they exploited with a breakout at St. Lo. on the 25th. July.
He is buried at Fontenay-Le-Pesnel War Cemetery, Tessel, Normandy, Grave 1V. D.17, and commemorated at St. Mary's Hayes.

27

DINES Joseph Frederick

Marine PLY/X 107201 Royal Marines, who died on Thursday, 13th. May, 1943 aged 18.
He was the son of Hannah Dines and stepson of J. Smith, of Hayes.
He was serving at H.M.S. *Condor*, a Royal Naval Air Station at Arbroath, Angus, close to Dundee.
His death certificate states he died "on War Service" but does not give any other details.
He is buried at Hayes (St. Mary's) Churchyard, Hayes.

DODSON Arthur Frederick

Sapper 5121591 723 Artisan Works Company, Royal Engineers, who died on Thursday, 6th
April, 1944 aged 22.
He was the son of Herbert and Mabel Dodson; husband of Doris Irene Dodson. of Hayes.
He was wounded in the fighting near Monte Cassino when the Allies were trying to breach the
Gustav Line, link up with the Anzio Beachhead and advance on Rome.
Bari in the south was an important supply base and also had several hospitals in one of which
Arthur died.
He is buried at Bari War Cemetery, Italy. Grave X1. C. 19.

ELLIOTT Edward Lawrence

Private 13019348 1/4th. Battalion, Hampshire Regiment, who died on Saturday, 16th. September,
1944 aged 39.
He was the son of George E. and Emily C. Elliott; husband of Ruby V. Elliott, of Hayes.
The 1/4th. Battalion with the 5th. and 2nd. Hants formed the 128th. Infantry Brigade of the 46th.
Infantry Division. Edward died during the advance from Ancona to Rimini (which broke the *Gothic*
Line) and in the heavy fighting around Rimini which was taken by the Allies on the 21st. September.
He is buried at Gradara War Cemetery, Italy. Grave 11. D. 7, and is commemorated at .St. Mary's,
Hayes'

ELLIOTT William Josiah

Aircraftman 2nd. Class 1285509 R.A.F.V.R. who died on Monday, 27th. October, 1941 aged 26.
He was the son of Charles and Margaret Elliott; husband of Clarice Margaret Elliott, of Hayes
He died at the R.A.F. Depot Hospital, Uxbridge of a cerebral haemorrhage and chronic nephritis.
He is buried at Uxbridge (Hillingdon) Cemetery, Row N.D. Grave 25.

ELLIS D.M.

Although commemorated at St. Mary's, Hayes, unfortunately I have not been able to trace this
person

ELLIS Richard Hall

Corporal 4621233 6th. Battalion, Black Watch (Royal Highlanders), who died on Thursday, 9th.
November, 1944 aged 29.
He was the son of John G. and Francis Ellis; husband of Edna Ellis, of Hayes.
The 6th Battalion with the 2nd. Royal Fusiliers and the 1st. Royal West Kents formed the 12th.
Infantry Brigade of the 4th. Infantry Division which arrived in Italy on the 6th. March, 1944.
Richard died in the heavy fighting, in appalling weather, between Rimini and Ravenna in
October-December 1944. Forli was taken in November.
He is buried at Forli War Cemetery, Italy. Grave V11. C. 23.

EVANS Henry Ernest
Ordinary Seaman P/JX 259339 H.M.S. *Victory*, Royal Navy, who died on Sunday, 11th. May, 1941 aged 21.
He was the son of Percy P. and Ellen L. Evans of Hayes End; husband of May Florence Evans.
His mother was living in May, 1941 at 8, Purcell Street, Shoreditch and he died as a result of an air raid at this address. H.M.S. Victory was not a ship but a shore base. In fact there were may shore bases and transit units with this name, and I am not able to locate the precise one in which he was serving. His death certificate states "he died due to war operations".
He is buried at the City of London Cemetery, Essex. Ref. 413. Grave 101481.

EVANS Thomas
Private 6147593 11th. Battalion, East Surrey Regiment, who died on Saturday, 26th. April, 1941 aged 27.
He was the son of Tom and Ada Evans, of Cranmer Road, Hayes End; husband of Winnie Evans.
He died in a air raid at Liverpool Street. Dover, Kent.
He is buried at Hayes and Harlington (Cherry Lane) Cemetery, Sec C. 1. Grave G. 31, and is commemorated at St. Mary's, Hayes.

EXELL Henry James
Fusilier 6468344 8th. Battalion, Royal Fusiliers (City of London Regiment), who died on Saturday, 11th. March, 1944 aged 27.
He was the son of William J. and Rose Exell; husband of Evelyn Doris Exell, of Hayes.
The 8th. Battalion was part of the 1st. London Infantry Brigade of the 56th. London Infantry Division who had been sent to Italy on 9th. September, 1943 and who took part in the landings at Salerno.
They were then transferred from the Cassino front to the beachhead at Anzio in January, 1944. He was taken prisoner but died of his wounds in captivity.
He is buried at Padua War Cemetery, Italy. Grave 111. B. 1. Padua is now called Padova and is just west of Venice.

FARR George William
Driver 10676315 Royal Electrical and Mechanical Engineers, who died on Wednesday, 14th. April, 1943 aged 27.
He was the son of George and Anne L. Farr; husband of Ivy Eileen Gillian Farr, of Hayes.
Enfidaville was taken by 8th. Army on the 19th. April, 1943 and George died in the battle for this town. Having done this the Allies were then ready for the final act in North Africa. The Axis had retreated to the north-east corner of Tunisia and the 1st and 8th. Armies launched their final offensive. They entered Tunis on the 7th. May and General *Von Arnim* surrendered his German and Italian troops.
The British had suffered 38,000 casualties in the Tunisian Campaign, of which 6,000 were fatal.
He is buried at Enfidaville War Cemetery, Tunisia. Grave V1. F. 27, and commemorated at St. Mary's Hayes. Enfidaville is a 100 kms. south of Tunis.

FELL James Anthony
Flight Sergeant 1471950 R.A.F.V.R. who died on Friday, 6th. October, 1944 aged 21.
He was the husband of Phyllis Beatrice Fell, of Hayes End.
He was a Wireless Operator / Air Gunner flying Lancaster 1 s with 106 Squadron of 5 Group based at Metheringham, Lincs. They took off at 1745 hrs. to bomb Bremen and are believed to have crashed in the sea. There were no survivors of the crew of eight. Six, including James, are commemorated on the Runnymede Memorial. Panel 217 and the Flight Engineer and Rear Gunner

are both buried at Becklington War Cemetery, Germany. James is also commemorated at St. Mary's, Hayes.

253 aircraft were despatched to carry out the last of 32 attacks on Bremen. The raid was an outstanding success and 1092 tons of bombs were dropped. Bremen was not attacked for the rest of the war. Five Lancasters were lost.

FETHERSTON Hugh Henry

Sergeant 1293338 R.A.F.V.R. who died on Thursday, 26th. March, 1942 aged 25.

He was the son of Henry and Mary Fetherston; husband of Ena Fetherston, of Hayes.

He was Air Gunner flying Manchester twin engined bombers (forerunner of the Lancaster) with 61 Squadron of 5 Group based at Woolfox Lodge, Lincs. They took off at 2110 hrs. to bomb Essen in the Ruhr. They were shot down by a night-fighter of NJG1 squadron and crashed 2209 hrs, at Wertherbruch, 8 kms. WSW of Bocholt. All are buried in Collective Grave 22. F. 1-5. at the Reichswald War Cemetery, Kleve, Nordrhein-Westfalen, Germany. He is commemorated at St. Mary's, Hayes.

254 aircraft were despatched and 9 were lost. The bombing was not accurate due to decoy fires being made at Rheinburg. Only seven of the recently introduced Lancasters were available for this raid.

FISHER David

Serjeant 6137964 2nd. Battalion, King's Shropshire Light Infantry, who died on Thursday, 1st. March, 1945 aged 34.

He was the son of Sam and Florence Fisher; husband of Ena Lilian Fisher, of Hayes.

The 2nd. Battalion was part of the 185th. Infantry Brigade of the 3rd. Infantry Division. They moved up to relieve the 15th. Scottish Division who had been clearing the Reichswald (Please see Frank **BOWGETT**) in Operation *Veritable*. They assembled in a concentration area north of Goch and were given the task of taking the town of Kervenheim.

From the book "Monty's Ironsides" by Patrick *Delaforce*

"Food came up at midnight and at 0900 hrs, the attack was renewed. Lt. Aldridge and Sgt. *Fisher* of the Pioneer company were killed by mortar fire. He, Aldridge would dodge about the battlefield in his jeep or on foot, ignoring completely shelling or mines, helping to evacuate the wounded, and doing all the odd jobs of the battle."

On the 5th. March the Division had completed its task. Now for the Rhine.

He is buried at the Reichswald Forest War Cemetery. Kleve, Nordrhein-Westfalen, Germany. Grave 62. F. 18, and commemorated at St. Mary's, Hayes.

FLEMING Horace Vivian

Ordinary Seaman D/JX 238469 H.M.S. *Jaguar*, Royal Navy, who died on Friday, 26th, March, 1942. He was the husband of Emily Violet Fleming, of Southall.

H.M.S. *Jaguar* was a destroyer of the *Javelin* class built in 1938 displacing 1760 tons and armed with 6 * 4.7 in guns, 10 * 21 inch torpedo tubes, and had a speed of 36 knots. She had a complement of 183.

Jaguar was escorting the oiler *Slavol* to Tobruk, Libya, where the oiler was to refuel the 5th. Destroyer Flotilla. At 0445 hrs just off Sidi Barrani the *Jaguar* was struck by two torpedoes fired by U 652 and sank at once. 53 survivors were rescued by the South African Anti-Submarine whaler *Klo*nut but 130 were lost including Horace. Two hours later the U 652 sank the *Slavol*.

Another resident of Hillingdon who died in this ship, was Petty Officer George **HUGHES** of Harefield.

Horace is commemorated on the Plymouth Naval Memorial. Panel 67. Column 2. and at St. Mary's, Hayes.

FOSKETT William James
Firewatcher who died on Saturday, 10th. May, 1941 aged 20.
He was the son of Mr. and Mrs. James William Foskett, of 71. Keith Road, Hayes; husband of M.V.R. Foskett, of the same address.
He died as a result of enemy bombing at 11, Queen Victoria Street, City of London.
He is commemorated at St. Mary's, Hayes.

FRASER Robert William
Sergeant 616009 R.A.F. who died on Thursday, 3rd. February, 1944 aged 23.
He was the son of Robert and Margaret Fraser; husband of Isobel Fraser, of Mannock, Dumfriesshire.
He was a Fitter 2E serving with 159 Squadron who were flying Liberator 111 s from Digri airfield which is north west of Calcutta.
Robert died of natural causes and is buried at Ranchi War Cemetery, Grave 9. F. 4, Ranchi is a town 400 kms. north-west of Calcutta and there are over 700 Commonwealth servicemen buried there. He is commemorated at St. Mary's, Hayes.

FRIPP Horace John
Ordinary Seaman C/JX 319331 H.M.S. *Achates*, Royal Navy, who died on Thursday, 31st. December, 1942.
He was the son of Ernest G. and Lilian Fripp, of Hayes.
H.M.S. *Achates* was an "A" Class destroyer of 1350 tons displacement, armed with 4 * 4.7 guns, 8 torpedo tubes with a speed of 35 knots. She was part of a destroyer force escorting a convoy to the North Russian ports, when at about 9.30 a.m. off Bear Island she was fired on from astern by the German heavy cruiser *Hipper* and this was followed by salvos from the pocket-battleship *Lutzow* and several destroyers. The *Onslow* now led the small force of destroyers against the attackers and a sharp action commenced in the semi-darkness of the Artic Circle, amid frequent snow showers. The *Achates* was hit forward by 8 inch shells early in the action, followed by a direct hit on the bridge which killed the captain, and everyone stationed there, except two sailors who were wounded. The next hit was in the boiler room and the vessel could no longer maintain steam. She was then hit repeatedly from six thousand yards range, down to almost zero. She finally turned over and sank in three minutes, taking with her 113 of her crew including Horace. There were only 80 survivors, who were picked up by the trawler *Northern Gem*.
With the action continuing, the British ships laid a smoke screen under cover of which the convoy turned away. They then drove off four determined attacks by the enemy, sinking the destroyer *Hermann Schoemann*. But help was at hand, the British medium cruisers *Sheffield* and *Jamaica* arrived and sank the German destroyer *Friedrick Eckoldt*. The German forces now broke off and withdrew.
The convoy reached its destination without loss or damage to a single merchant ship.
He is commemorated on the Chatham Naval Memorial. Panel 57.2, and at St. Mary's, Hayes.

FROGLEY John Edward
Sergeant R.A.F.V.R. 770058 who died on Friday, 5th. May, 1944
He was serving as a clerk in No. 9. Operations Room, India, and died of natural causes.
He is buried at Calcutta (Bhowanipore) Cemetery, India. Plot L. Grave 63. and commemorated at St. Mary's, Hayes.

FROST Eric Roland
Leading Stoker P/KX 81259 H.M. Submarine *Odin*, Royal Navy, who died on Thursday, 27th. June, 1940 aged 26.
He was the son of Arthur G. and Jessie V. Frost, of Hayes.
H.M.S. *Odin* was a submarine of the *Oberon* class built in 1929, of 1300/1800 tons displacement, with 8 * 21 inch torpedo tubes,
Taranto was the principal base for the Italian Navy, and the approaches were always well guarded. *Odin* was a large submarine, recently arrived in the Mediterranean from the Far East, and she left Malta on 11th. June for a patrol, right to the *Regia Marina's* back yard. At 2321 hrs. on the 13th. the Italian escort *Strale*, on anti submarine patrol in the Gulf of Taranto, sighted a large submarine - H.M.S. *Odin* - that she attacked with a torpedo (which was seen to strike), gunfire and depth-charges. At 9157 hrs. on the 14th. the escort *Baleno* sighted a submarine in the same area, 9 miles from the position of the *Strale's* attack. She then attacked with depth-charges. Aerial survey of the scene on the 14th. revealed an oil slick that eventually covered ten miles. None of the *Odin's* crew of fifty three survived the sinking.
He is commemorated on the Portsmouth Naval Memorial. Panel 41. Column 3.

FRY Leslie Ernest
Lance Corporal 6149139 The Hallamshire Battalion, York and Lancaster Regiment, who died on Tuesday, 26th. September, 1944 aged 29.
He was the son of Percy L. and Eliza J. Fry; husband of Thelma Norah Victoria Fry, of Hayes.
The Hallamshire Battalion was part of the 146th. Brigade of the 49th West Riding Infantry Division, known as the *Polar Bears* because of their emblem. They had landed in Normandy on the 10th June, D Day +4 and had advanced across France and Belgium.
Operation *Market-Garden*, the attempt to take the bridges over the Lower Rhine had started on the 19th. September and ended on the 25th. with the withdrawal from Arnhem. The *Polar Bears* were at Geel which is 46 kms. east of Antwerp and on the left flank of the *Market Garden* ground advance to Arnhem. Leslie died in the fighting on this front, the day after the Battle for Arnhem had ended.
He is buried at Geel War Cemetery, Antwerp, Belgium. Grave 11. C. 11, and commemorated at St. Mary's, Hayes.

FRY William Arthur
Deck Hand S.S. *Royal Crown* (Newcastle-on-Tyne), Merchant Navy, who died on Tuesday, 30th. January, 1940 aged 23.
He was the son of Francis and Martha Fry. of Hayes.
The *Royal Crown* was a Hall Bros. steamship of 4,300 tons displacement built in 1927, with a speed of 10 knots. On the 30th. January, she was bombed by German aircraft and forced to run ashore near Lowestoft. In the attack three officers were killed. The Captain and 18 officers and men (including William) were drowned in their efforts to reach shore in a heavy sea. The vessel was subsequently re-floated. but was captured and sunk by the German battlecruiser *Gneisenau* in the North Atlantic, on the 16th. March, 1941 with the new crew being taken prisoner.
He and his comrades are buried at Lowestoft (Beccles Road) Cemetery, Lowestoft, Suffolk. Sec. O.A. Collective Grave 518, and he is commemorated at St. Mary's, Hayes.

FULLER Edward Percival
Gunner 1804362 80 Heavy Anti-Aircraft Regiment, Royal Artillery, who died on Monday, 8th. November, 1943 aged 32.
He was the son of William Edmund and Ethel L. Fuller, of Hayes.

The 80th. H.A.A. Regiment had been part of 1st. Army who landed in Algeria in November, 1942 and drove the Axis forces out of North Africa. They were transferred to the Eighth Army and took part in the liberation of Sicily
They then crossed into Italy and were now advancing up the toe of Italy to link up with the Allied troops due to land at Salerno on the early hours of the 9th. Edward was killed in this advance. After Naples fell on the 30th all the Allied soldiers who had fallen in the recent fighting were reburied at Salerno War Cemetery, Italy. His Grave is V1. B. 30.

FURNESS John
Chief Stoker P/KX 76725 H.M.S. *Penelope*, Royal Navy, who died on Friday, 18th. February, 1944 aged 37.
He was the son of William and Marie Furness; husband of Ivy Furness, of Hayes.
H.M.S. *Penelope* was a cruiser of the *Arethusa* class, displacing 5,300 tons, armed with 6 * six inch guns. She endured many air attacks in the Mediterranean and was affectionately known as H.M.S. *Pepperpot*, because of the damage she suffered.
She was torpedoed 25 miles west of Naples by U. 410 and sank 10 minutes later after a major explosion in the aft magazine. Four hundred and fifteen men were lost including John, and there were only eighty-five survivors.
He is commemorated on the Portsmouth Naval Memorial. Panel 85. Column 1, and at St. Mary's, Hayes.

GARDINER A.J.
Although commemorated at St. Mary's, Hayes, unfortunately I have not been able to trace this person

GEORGE Eric Raymond
Leading Airman S/FX 2232 H.M.S. *Daedalus*, Royal Navy, who died on Sunday, 7th. March, 1943 aged 22.
He was the son of Frederick G. and Violet A. George, of Hayes.
H.M.S. *Daedalus*, was a large Royal Navy Air Station at Lee-on-Solent, Hants.
His body was found on Haslar beach and his death certificate states he died "due to war operations". No other details are shown, but he probably died of drowning.
He is buried at Haslar Royal Naval Cemetery, Hants. Grave E. 63. 3, and commemorated at St. Mary's, Hayes, and St. Peter's and St. Paul's, Harlington.

GILES Donald Aubrey Newdigate
Gunner 6153800 78 (The Duke of Lancaster's Own Yeomanry) Medium Regiment, Royal Artillery, who died on Sunday, 30th, April, 1944 aged 20.
He was the son of Herbert R. and Phoebe C. Giles. of Hayes. Please note his brother Kenneth below.
The 78th. was part of the Army artillery of 8th. Army who were trying to make the big breakthrough in the Gustav Line at Monte Cassino. Donald died in the preliminary fighting before Operation Diadem started on the 11th. May. After five days the Germans were in full retreat and did not stop until they were north of Rome, which fell on the 5th. June.
He is buried at Cassino War Cemetery, Italy. Grave V111. E. 17.

GILES Kenneth Arthur Robert
Leading Aircraftsman 1430913 R.A.F.V.R. who died on Thursday, 13th. September, 1945 aged 25.
He was a Flight Mechanic (Engineer) serving with the Mediterranean and Middle East
Communication Squadron based at Kabrit in the Suez Canal Zone. He was admitted to No.5. RAF
Hospital, Abassia, dangerously ill on the 12th. September and died the next day of tuberculosis.
He is buried at Heliopolis War Cemetery, Cairo, Egypt. Grave 6. H. 4.

GILES William Stanley
Lance Corporal 14764346 2nd. Battalion, Scots Guards, who died on Sunday, 11th. March, 1945
aged 18.
He was the son of John and Agnes Giles, of Hayes.
The 2nd. Battalion was part of the 5th. Guards Armoured Brigade of the Guards Armoured Division
who had landed in Normandy on the 30th. June, 1944.
They had advanced through France, Belgium, Holland having taken part in all the key battles of the
campaign. They had now crossed the Rhine and were taking part in the Battle of the Rhineland in
which William was killed..
Peace in Europe was only two months away.
He is buried at Reichswald Forest War Cemetery, Kleve, Nordrhein-Westfalen, Germany. Grave 43.
C.16, and commemorated at St. Mary's, Hayes.

GILLICK Thomas Francis
Gunner 1602118 191 Battery, 64 Light Anti-Aircraft Regiment, Royal Artillery, who died on Friday,
11th. April, 1941 aged 27.
He was the son of Thomas and Ethel L. Gillick of South Lane, New Malden. Surrey: husband of
Martha Elizabeth Gillick, of Hayes.
He died of cancer at Middlesex Hospital. In civilian life he was an Advertising Agent's Traveller.
He is buried at Kingston-upon-Thames Cemetery, Surrey. Grave 2391.

GLEED Robert George
Ordinary Seaman LT/JX 322654 *H.M.B.Y. Minesweeper 2077*, Royal Naval Patrol Service, who died
on Wednesday, 25th. October, 1944.
H.M. Brooklyn Yard Minesweepers named after the yard where they were designed, were made of
wood to counter the enemy's use of magnetic mines. They displaced 210 tons, were diesel powered
and had a speed of 13 knots. She was armed with 1 * 3 inch and 2 * 20 mm. guns.
The Germans had laid dense minefields to impede Allied progress in liberating Greece, and
especially Piraeus. A large fleet of sweepers was engaged in this very dangerous clearance; two
flotillas of "*Algerines*", a number of BYMSs, GYMSs (crewed by the Greek Navy), and Motor
Launches. In the operation three of the Greek vessels were sunk, together with ML 870 and two
"Algerines" being damaged, mostly in the initial clearance sweep of the channel into the Gulf of
Athens. Hundreds of mines were cleared, mostly of the moored contact variety. A little later, in
the same area, Robert's ship the BYMS 2077 was sunk, and all except seven of her crew were lost,
when she struck a moored mine on the edge of the channel being swept.
He is commemorated on the Lowestoft Naval Memorial Panel 15. Column 1, and at St. Mary's,
Hayes.

GODFREY Alf
Serjeant 780486 17 Field Regiment, Royal Artillery, who died on Monday, 9th. August, 1943 aged
32.
He was the son of Dennis and Ada Godfrey; husband of Ann Francis Godfrey, of Hayes.

The 17th. Field Regiment was part of the Divisional artillery of the 78th. Infantry (Battleaxe) Division. They had landed in Algeria in November 1942 and had help drive the Axis out of Africa. On the 10th. July Sicily was invaded by combined American and British forces. The Battleaxe Division was held in reserve and when *Montgomery* realised his advance on the east side of Sicily was being held up by the Herman Goering Division he sent for them (reluctantly, they were not his favourite division) and they arrived on the 25th. July; the same day that *Mussolini* was dismissed. They helped take the town of Centuripe and advanced on the west side of Mount Etna. Alf died in the attack on Randazzo which started on the 9th. August. Mount Macerone was then taken and they linked up with the US 9th Division advancing from the north. This was the end of the Division's fighting in Sicily, which was by the end of August in Allied hands.
He is buried at Catania War Cemetery, Sicily. Grave 11. J. 27.

GOOCH Edward James
Lance Bombardier 1111348 6th. Regiment, Royal Horse Artillery, who died on Tuesday, 22nd. July, 1941 aged 28.
He was the son of Noah and Emily E. Gooch; husband of Marjorie M. Gooch, of Church Road, Hayes.
He died from internal injuries and shock caused by being crushed on the overturning of a Military vehicle at Garrowby Hill, Bishop Wilton, Nr. Pocklington, East Yorkshire.
In civilian life he was a labourer in a Chemical Dye Works.
He is buried at Hayes (St. Mary's) Churchyard Extension and is commemorated on the Church Memorial.

GOWER Herbert George (known as Phil)
Marine Ch/X110242 Royal Marines, who died on Monday, 23rd. August, 1943 aged 20.
He was the son of Herbert H. and Edith K. Gower, of 146, Kings Road, Harrogate, Yorkshire.
He was serving with No.42 R.M. Commando and died of natural causes at Lymington and District Hospital, Hants.
He is buried at Hanwell Cemetery Plot 238 Grave 12898, and commemorated at St. Mary's, Hayes.

GRAVELL Leonard
Serjeant 3187845 2nd. Battalion, King's Own Scottish Borderers, who died on Wednesday, 19th. January, 1944 aged 26.
He was the son of Richard D. and Mary A. Gravell, of Hayes.
The 2nd. KOSB's had been in India since 1939, and now, with the 7/2 nd. Punjabs and 4/8 Gurkhas formed the 89th. Indian Infantry Brigade. It had been the practice since the Indian Mutiny for one battalion in an Indian Brigade to be British.
They moved to the Arakan in September 1943 and were taking part in the offensive that had started in November. He died in the fighting to take the port of Moungdaw, the capture of which would enable supplies to be brought by ship from Calcutta. The fighting in the Arakan did not end until the 3rd. May, 1944 when the Japanese moved their forces to Imphal.
When a British soldier died in the jungle he was buried and an officer made a note in the Company records of the map reference so that he could be reburied at a later date. Unfortunately this was not always possible and in Leonard's case he is commemorated on the Rangoon Memorial, Myanmar, (Burma). Face 10.

GRAY Walter Thomas
Private 5731278 1/4th. Battalion, Essex Regiment, who died on Saturday, 7th. October, 1944 aged 29.
He was the son of Stanley and Georgina Gray, of Hayes.
The 1/4th. Essex with the 1/6 Rajputs and 1/9 Gurkhas formed the 5th. Indian Infantry Brigade of the 4th. Indian Infantry Division who arrived in Egypt in June, 1942. They had fought at El Alamein, in Tripolatania, Tunisia and arrived in Italy on the 16th. November. 1943. They had then taken part in the Cassino battles and advanced northward to the Coriano Ridge.
The Coriano Ridge was the last important ridge in the way of the Allied advance in the Adriatic sector in the autumn of 1944. Its capture was the key to Rimini and the river Po. German Parachute and Panzer troops, aided by bad weather, resisted all attacks between the 4th and 12th. September. On the night of the 12th. the 1st. British Armoured Division and the 5th. Canadian Armoured Division attacked. They were successful in taking the ridge, but it marked the beginning of a week that experienced the heaviest fighting since Cassino, the Eighth Army losing daily 150 killed. Walter died in the fighting in following up the success of the capture of the ridge.
He is buried at the Coriano Ridge War Cemetery, Italy. Grave XV111. A. 4, and commemorated at St. Peter's and St. Paul's, Harlington.

GREEN Gerald Frank
Private 4756098 1/5th. Battalion, Sherwood Foresters (Notts. and Derby Regiment), who died on Tuesday 12th. September, 1944 aged 30.
He was the son of Ernest and Violet J. Green, of York Avenue, Hayes End.
The Sherwood Foresters was part of the 55th. Infantry Brigade of the 18th, Division who arrived in Singapore on the 29th. January 1942 and were taken prisoner when the Allies surrendered on the 15th, February. (Please see note below)
He has no known grave and was killed when the vessel in which he was being transported was sunk by Allied forces. In civilian life he was a labourer.
He is commemorated on the Singapore Memorial. Column 71, and at St. Mary's Hayes.

18th Infantry Division

Roosevelt had agreed with *Churchill* to supply U.S. troopships and escorts to transport this mechanised division to the Middle East. They sailed from England in early November 1941 for Halifax, Newfoundland. There they transferred to the American ships and left Halifax on the 10th. November.
Whilst rounding the Cape of Good Hope, on the 8th. December the news broke that the Japanese had bombed Pearl Harbour and invaded Malaya. The 53rd. Brigade (5th. and 6th. Norfolks, and 2nd, Cambridgeshires) was therefore switched to Singapore and the 54th. Brigade (4th. Norfolks, 4th. and 5th. Suffolks) and 55th. Brigade (5th. Beds and Herts., 1/5 th. Sherwood Foresters, and 1st. Cambridgeshires) to Bombay. The 53rd. Brigade arrived in Singapore on the 14th. January 1942 after 11 weeks at sea
Such was the desperation of the Allied Forces that after three days and not aclimatised, they were sent to Johore and suffered heavy casualties. The other two Brigades which were at Bombay were now sent to Singapore and arrived on the 29th. January, just 18 days before the surrender. *Churchill* was not in favour of sending them to Singapore as he did not believe in reinforcing failure and foresaw what was going to happen to the rest of the division. But such was the pressure from the Australian Government that he decided to send them to retain the support of the Australians on a world wide basis.

After withdrawing from Johore to the island of Singapore the Allied forces prepared themselves for the final assault from the Japanese across the Straits. Lt. General *Percival* who was in charge of the Allied forces decided that the main Japanese thrust would come in the north-east and he decided to place the three brigades of the fresh but non aclimatised 18th. Division there. But the Japanese struck in the north west and swept through the western part of the island outflanking the 18th. Division. On the 15th. February *Percival* surrendered, and all the surviving Allied troops were taken into captivity. The Japanese had beaten their target date for Singapore's capture by thirty days.

GRIFFITHS Frank
Petty Officer Stoker D/KX 83453 H.M.S. *Itchen*, Royal Navy, who died on Thursday, 23rd. September, 1943 aged 38.
He was the son of Mr. and Mrs. Frank Griffiths; husband of Joan Muriel Griffiths, of Hayes.
H.M.S. *Itchen* was a *River* class frigate of 1,370 tons and armed with 2 * 4 inch guns, with a crew of 140. The *Itchen* together with the Canadian destroyer *St. Croix*, the frigate *Lagan*, the corvette *Polyanthus*, and the Canadian corvette *Morden*, were escorting the west-bound convoy ON 292 south of Greenland. This convoy was selected by Admiral *Doenitz* to renew the Battle of the Atlantic following the defeats of the U-boats in May. This time the U-boats had a new weapon, the T5 or acoustic torpedo (*Gnat* in British parlance). *Lagan* was the first victim of this new weapon. She was torpedoed at 0305 hrs. had her stern blown off by U 270 and she had to be towed to the UK by the tug *Destiny*, and was later scrapped
Fourteen hours after the *Lagan* was torpedoed the *St. Croix* was torpedoed at 1758 hrs. by U 305. She lay dead in the water until a second attack by the same submarine sank her. Eighty of her crew were lost and the survivors picked up by the *Itchen*.
Polyanthus was the third escort to be torpedoed. At 2316 hrs. she was sunk by U 952 using a T.5. The little corvette sank with the loss of 84 lives.
Itchen was the first British frigate to be sunk during the Second World War and the fourth escort to be sank in the battles around this convoy. At 2355 hrs. she was torpedoed by U. 666. The forward magazine blew up and the ship sank almost immediately. She was carrying eighty survivors from the *St. Croix* as well as her own company but only three survived, two from the *Itchen*, the other from the *St. Croix*. Frank was lost with 147 of his comrades from the *Itchen*. Six merchant ships from this convoy were also lost.
He is commemorated on the Plymouth Naval Memorial. Panel 81. Column 3.

GRIFFITHS Leslie   DSO
Commander, R.N.R.D. (Royal Naval Reserve Decoration), Royal Naval Reserve H.M.S. *Yeoman*, Royal Naval Reserve who died on Wednesday, 19th. July, 1944 aged 43.
He was the son of Frank D. and Kate Griffiths of Hayes; husband of Mabel Griffiths   He was the holder of the Distinguished Service Order. (unfortunately I have not been able trace the details)
Leslie died at the Essex County Hospital, Wanstead after being hit by a V.1. Pilotless Bomb in Eagle Lane, Wanstead, His wife Mabel was also killed in the same incident, His home address is given as Tudor Drive, Kingston-upon-Thames, and he was the Chief Officer of the New Zealand Shipping Company.
He is buried at Woodford (Roding) Lane) Cemetery, Essex. Grave 1.

GROVES Frederick
Gunner 1550169 95 Battery, 48 Light Anti-Aircraft Regiment, Royal Artillery, who died on Wednesday, 7th. March, 1945 aged 28
He was the son of Mr. and Mrs. H. Groves. of South Ealing; husband of Mrs.T.E. Groves, of Hayes.

The 48th. Light Anti-Aircraft Regiment left the U.K. for overseas (probably the Middle East) on the 6th. December, 1941. While at sea they were diverted to Java, and arrived there on the 3rd. February, 1942.
The Japanese who had already conquered Malaya and Singapore, now invaded Java and he was taken prisoner on the 12th. March
He died on a Japanese ship bound for Japan which was sunk by American Air or Submarine forces. He is commemorated on the Singapore Memorial. Column 19.

GUTTRIDGE Raymond Albert

Serjeant 4799484 Lincolnshire Regiment, who died on Sunday, 14th. July, 1940 aged 26.
He was the son of Victor L. and Sarah A. Guttridge; husband of Edith Vera Guttridge, of Hayes.
He died in the Memorial Hospital, Cirencester after being involved in a road traffic accident at Victoria Road, Cirencester, when testing a motor cycle. His address on the death certificate is given as Erlanger Road, New Cross, London.
He is buried at Cirencester Cemetery, Glos. E. Row N. Grave 1.

HACKWELL William Thomas

Rifleman 6844792 2nd. Battalion, King's Royal Rifle Corps, who died on Sunday, 26th. May, 1940 aged 29.
He was the son of Henry B. and Martha Hackwell, of Hayes.
The German Blitzkrieg which started on May 10th. 1940 reached the Atlantic Coast on the 20th., and the Germans started to roll up the coast, trying to capture all the seaports to prevent the British Expeditionary Force escaping to England.
Dunkirk was the only port open to the BEF, and it was decided to send forces to hold Boulogne and Calais. On the 22nd May the Guards Brigade landed at Boulogne and attempted to hold the port. But the 2nd. Panzer Division began their attack at 5 p.m. the same day, supported by the Luftwaffe. The following evening the Guards were ordered to withdraw and embark from the blazing harbour. Some embarked, some were captured, and some held out for another day before being finally overwhelmed and the port was in German hands by the 25th. May.
Also on the 22nd. May a battalion with a small number of tanks was sent to Calais, but the town was soon invested by the 6th. Panzer Division. The next day the 30th. Brigade comprising the 2nd, Battalion and the 1st. Rifle Battalion was sent in as reinforcements. The Germans then began their final onslaught, having brought in the 10th. and 1st. Panzer Divisions. On the 24th. Calais was attacked on three sides. The British commander was told to fight to the last, there would be no evacuation "for the sake of Allied solidarity". They had never had the explosives to blow the bridges over the canals. Next day the Germans drove the defenders into the northern part of the town. There was no surrender, there was no evacuation, broken into small parties the gallant commander and troops of 30th. Brigade were finally overwhelmed.
William died on the 26th. and Duncan **Moore,** of Ickenham and the same regiment, on the 25th. William is buried at Calais Southern Cemetery, Pas de Calais. Plot O. Grave 29, and commemorated at St. Mary's Hayes.

HALDANE Sydney John

Sergeant 551723 R.A.F. who died on Friday, 30th. August, 1940 aged 19.
He was the son of Herbert and Kathleen M. D. Haldane, of Hayes.
He was a Wireless Operator / Air Gunner flying Wellington 1C s with 214 Squadron based at Stradishall, Suffolk. They took off to bomb Berlin but crashed near Halle (Gelderland) 9 kms. ENE of Doetinchem, Holland. All six of the crew were killed and are buried in a Collective grave at the

Zelhem (Halle) Protestant Cemetery, Gelderland, Holland.   Sydney is commemorated at St. Mary's, Hayes.
120 aircraft were sent and 3 were lost.   This raid probably changed the outcome of the Battle of Britain.   *Hitler* and *Goering*, furious that despite their promises to the German people, Berlin had been bombed, switched their bombers from the Fighter Command airfields to London, which most historians believe lost them the battle.

HALL Richard John
Private 14575892 1st. Battalion, Hampshire Regiment, who died on Wednesday, 14th. June, 1944 aged 19.
He was the son of Richard and Alice Hall, of Harlington.
The 1st Hants. was part of the 231 Infantry Brigade of the 50th. Infantry (Northumberland) Division. They had been training in Norfolk and on D-Day they landed on Gold Beach, Normandy at 7.30 am. with the 1st. Dorsets.   They were on the extreme west flank of the British and Canadian forces and because they had the funnys (specialised tanks) they avoided the disaster of Omaha Beach,   See Spielberg's"Saving Sergeant Ryan",
There is a possibility that he was among the first English soldiers to "brew up" in Europe since 1940. After linking up with the U.S. forces they attacked Tilly-sur-Seulles (just north of Villers Bocage) and Richard was killed in this battle.
He is buried at Hottot-Les-Baques War Cemetery, Calvados.   Grave II. E. 4, and commemorated at St. Mary's, Harmondsworth.

HARCOURT Vernon Ralph Garcia   D.F.C.
Squadron Leader, 41790 R.A.F. who died on Friday, 21st. May, 1943 aged 25.
He was the son of Frederick J. and Emily G. Harcourt, of Willow Tree Lane, Yeading.
He was a pilot flying Mosquito 1V s with 139 Squadron of 2 Group from Horsham St. Faith, Norfolk.   He was leading a flight of four Mosquitos to attack the Engine Sheds at Orleans, France. They were hit by flak on the coast, the aircraft crashed and Vernon and his navigator W/O J. Friendly D.F.M. were both killed.   He had been awarded the Distinguished Flying Cross on the 7th. April, 1942 for his service in 108 Squadron, flying Wellingtons 1 C s and Liberator 11 s from Kabrit in the Suez Canal Zone.
He is buried at Dieppe Canadian War Cemetery, Hautot-sur-Mer, Seine-Maritime, France.   Grave H. 17.   He is commemorated on the Memorial at St. Mary's, Hayes, and at Bishopshalt School where he was a former pupil.

HARDY George William
Private 6147788 2nd Battalion, East Surrey Regiment, who died on Thursday, 5th. February, 1942 aged 28.
He was the son of Mr. and Mrs. G.C. Hardy of Hayes.
The 2nd. Battalion was part of the 1st. Malaya Infantry Brigade stationed in Malaya in 1941.   The Japanese invaded Siam and Malaya on the 8th. December, 1941 and proceeded to advance in two columns southward through Malaya.   The Commonwealth forces were not able to stop their advance and suffered heavy casualties.   So heavy were the losses, that on the 19th. December the East Surreys and the 1st. Leicesters were amalgamated into the British Battalion under the command of the 15th. Independent Indian Brigade.   But they continued to retreat and on the 1st. February 1942 withdrew across the causeway to the island of Singapore
He died on the 5th. in the preliminary fighting and artillery exchanges before the Japanese crossed the channel on the 8th. February.   Singapore surrendered on the 15th. and 130,000 Commonwealth troops became prisoners of the Japanese, to await the horrible conditions forced upon them.

He is commemorated on the Singapore Memorial Column 69, and at St. Mary's, Hayes.

HARPER Leonard Sidney
Driver T/14562999 63 (Airborne) Component. Company, Royal Army Service Corps, who died on
Tuesday, 19th. September, 1944 aged 29.
He was the son of Danny Harper; stepson of Mrs. M.A. Harper, of Harlington,.
The Airborne forces landed at Arnhem on the 17th. and he died two days later in the heavy fighting.
He is buried at Arnhem Oosterbeek War Cemetery, Gelderland, Holland. Grave 15. B. 15, and
commemorated at St. Peter's and St. Paul's, Harlington.
Please see note after Alexander **BAISDEN**

HARRIS Frederick James Dennis
Cadet 1st. Class, Air Training Corps, who died on Sunday, 30th. July, 1944 aged 18.
He was the son of Frederick and Elsie M. Harris, of York Avenue, Hayes.
He was a wireless technician, and as a cadet was a passenger in an aircraft which crashed at Home
Farm, North Bucks. The coroner was unable to find any reason for the crash.
He is buried at Oxford (Botley) Cemetery, Oxon. Plot 1/2. Grave 253, and commemorated at St.
Mary's, Hayes.

HARVEY D.I.
Although commemorated at St. Mary's, Hayes and St. Peter's and St.Paul's, Harlington,
unfortunately I have not been able to trace this person

HATHORN Reginald Kenneth William
Leading Air Fitter, L/FX 690882 H.M.S. *Goldfinch*, Royal Navy, who died on Friday, 5th. April,
1946 aged 23.
He was the son of Henry E. and Minnie E. Hathorn of Hayes.
H.M.S.. *Goldfinch* was the Naval Air Station at Ta Kali which had been taken over from the R.A.F.
The death certificate prepared by the Royal Navy is as informative as usual, and states that he "died
on War Service". No other details are given.
He is buried at Malta (Capuccini) Naval Cemetery, Malta. Plot E. Grave 39, and commemorated at
St. Mary's, Hayes.

HAYNES William George
Lance Corporal 4031623 1st. Battalion, Herefordshire Regiment, King's Shropshire Light Infantry,
who died on Friday, 4th. February, 1944 aged 28.
The 1st. Battalion was part of the 3rd. Infantry Brigade of the 1st. Infantry Division who moved to
Italy from South Africa in December, 1943. They then led the landings at Anzio. (See entry after T.
CLARE. William was killed in the German counter-attack which started on the 3rd.
He is buried at the Anzio War Cemetery, Grave 11. X. 6. and is commemorated at St. Mary's, Hayes.
and St. Peter's and St. Paul's, Harlington

HEALY Thomas Valentine
Volunteer 17th. Middlesex Battalion, Home Guard, who died on Friday, 28th. March, 1941 aged 45.
He was the son of James and Annie Healy, of Mountain Ash, Glamorgan; husband of Ada E. Healy,
of 50. Rosedale Avenue, Hayes.
At night he lost his way and walked into the canal and drowned. This took place at the Canal Dock,
Silverdale Road, Hayes.

He is buried at Hayes and Harlington (Cherry Lane) Cemetery. Sec. C.1. Grave Q. 9, and commemorated at St. Mary's, Hayes.

HEARNE Herbert Royson
Leading Aircraftman 1380334 R.A.F.V.R. who died on Monday, 7th. July, 1941 aged 21.
He was the son of John W. and Violet M. Hearne, of Harlington.
He was a trainee pilot with No.24 Elementary Flying Training School. He was flying a Miles Magister single engined elementary trainer with the pupil and instructor in tandem, when he collided with a Tiger Moth Biplane. The Magister crashed 1 1/2 miles north west of the relief landing ground at Barton Le Clay, which is just north of Luton.
He is buried at Hayes and Harlington (Harlington) Burial Ground, Grave G.27, and commemorated at St. Peter's and St. Paul's, Harlington.

HERON Stephen
Leading Aircraftman 1447899 R.A.F.V.R. who died on Friday, 23rd. July, 1943 aged 22.
He was the son of John and Ida E. Heron, of Hayes.
He was serving with 32 Squadron, who were flying Spitfire V C s based at Tingley, Algeria, (near Bone). It was very hot and the Squadron was very busy that day.
They were on an American lorry, when it swerved to avoid another vehicle, and they crashed into a tree. One branch killed Stephen outright and an L.A.C. Hilton was wounded and died later from his injuries.
He is buried at Bone War Cemetery, Annaba, Algeria. Grave I, C. 6. and commemorated at St. Mary's, Hayes.

HICKMAN Morris Fleming Alexander
Serjeant 1913258 Royal Engineers, who died on Wednesday, 3rd. March, 1943 aged 33.
He was the son of Flemyne and Aileen J. Hickman; husband of Eva Elizabeth Hickman, of Hayes.
He died of typhus and is buried at Tehran War Cemetery, Iran. Grave 6. C. 6. He is commemorated at St. Marys, Hayes.
Tehran War Cemetery contains the graves of 152 Commonwealth servicemen and 3 are from Hillingdon. The other two being Captain A. K.. Wade-Smith, of the Gurkhas and Northwood, and Private H.J. Shervill. of the Royal Sussex Regiment, and Hillingdon Heath.

HIPSEY Ronald
Serjeant 319123 7th. Queen's Own Hussars, Royal Armoured Corps, who died on Monday, 30th. March, 1942 aged 28,
He was the son of Edwin and Minnie M. M. Hipsey, of Hayes.
The 7th. Queens was part of the 7th. Armoured Brigade of the 7th. Armoured Division (the Desert Rats) and were fighting in Libya at the end of 1941, armed with 115 new American Stuart (Honey) light tanks. The Stuart had a crew of four, a speed of 36 m.p.h., weighed 12 tons and was armed with a 37 mm. gun and two machine guns. Although mainly used for reconnaissance in the desert they were used as a battle tank in the jungle.
They were sent to Singapore but following the Japanese successes they were diverted to Rangoon in Burma and arrived on the 20th. February, 1942. They were thrown into action immediately, but the fighting was going against the Allies and it was decided to abandon Rangoon and retreat northwards.
Ronald was a tank commander and died in the battle for Prome, when with another tank, he succeeded in breaking through the Japanese road block, and enable the column to escape. The battle for the vital oilfields started on the 11th. April and the Allies were again forced to withdraw, destroying as much oil field equipment as they could. They crossed the Chindwin on the 10th. May,

having had to destroy the 70 surviving tanks, which they could not get across the river. On the 15th. they reached India having carried out one of the longest and most difficult retreats in the annals of the British Army.

He is commemorated on the Rangoon Memorial, Burma (Myanmar) Face 1, and at St. Mary's, Hayes.

HOARE Albert John

Able Seaman P/J 98031 H.M.S. *Acasta*, Royal Navy, who died on Sunday, 9th. June, 1940.

The destroyer *Acasta* was built in 1927, displaced 1350 tons, was armed with four 4.7 inch guns. The aircraft carrier *Glorious* was heading back to the U.K. from Norway escorted by her and the destroyer *Ardent*. The *Glorious* was steaming at 17 knots and had no aircraft on patrol, and at 1600 hrs. spotted the two German battlecruisers *Scharnhorst* and *Gneisenau*. In perfect weather conditions they opened fire at 1631 hrs. No aircraft were flown off and despite both destroyers laying a smokescreen *Glorious* was hit in the forward upper hangar. This left a massive hole in the flight deck and started a fierce fire. Further hits followed and at 1730 hrs. the order was given to abandon ship, and at 1740 hrs. she rolled over and sank. 1157 of the crew and 41 R.A.F. personnel were lost and there was only 48 survivors.

When *Glorious* came under fire from the two German battlecruisers the *Ardent* moved out towards them at high speed, making smoke. She fired one salvo of eight torpedoes, but was then hit several times and sunk at 1728 hrs. 152 of the crew died, and there were only two survivors, picked up by a German seaplane on June 11th.

After *Ardent* sank, *Acasta* continued to engage the enemy ships though hopelessly outgunned and outranged. Even though she could have escaped behind the smokescreen the Captain decided to make one final torpedo attack. One torpedo hit the *Scharnhorst*, but during this attack the *Acasta* was hit and sank just after 1810. hrs. 160 of the crew died including Walter and there was only one survivor.

He is commemorated on the Portsmouth Naval Memorial. Panel 38. Column 3, and at St. Peter's and St. Paul's Harlington.

Also serving in the *Acasta* were Walter **Barnes** of Yiewsley and William **Hobbs**, of Harmondsworth

HOLMES Kenneth John

Sergeant 1604724 R.A.F.V.R. who died on Friday, 16th. March, 1945.

He was an Air Bomber flying :Lancaster 1 s with 625 Squadron of 1 Group from Kelstern, Lincs. They took off at 1746 hrs. to attack Nurenberg. The were shot down over the target area and the crew of seven are all buried at Durnbach Cemetery, Bad Tolz, Collective grave 11. J. 12-15. Durnbach is 48 kms. south of Munich. He is commemorated at St. Mary's, Hayes.

The rear gunner Sgt. E.K. Day, at 41 was amongst the oldest airmen killed on Bomber Command operations, and was more than twice the age of one of the other gunners.

277 Lancasters and 16 Mosquitoes were sent and 24 were lost due to enemy night fighters. which found the bomber stream on its way to the target. Damage was so considerable that this the last Bomber Command raid of the war on Nurenberg.

HOPKINS David Reginald

Gunner 14269237 124 Heavy Anti-Aircraft Regiment, Royal Artillery, who died on Saturday, 25th. December 1943 aged 21.

He was the son of John T. and Margaret L. Hopkins, of Lime Grove, Hayes.

He died at St. Martin's Hospital, Bath, of pulmonary infection, and appendicitis.

He is buried at Hayes and Harlington (Cherry Lane) Cemetery. Sec. G.1. Grave M.12.

HORSPOOL William

Private 5731535 4th. Battalion, Dorsetshire Regiment, who died on Monday, 10th. July, 1944 aged 31.

He was the husband of Gladys Georgina Horspool, of Lightwater, Surrey.

The 4th. Dorsets was part of the 130th. Brigade of the 43rd. Wessex Infantry Division who had landed in Normandy on the 24th. June.

For details of his death please see entry after **Kenneth BEEBE.**

He is commemorated on the Bayeux Memorial, Calvados, France. Panel 15. Column 3. and at St. Peter's and St. Paul's, Harlington.

HOWE Arthur Edward

Craftsman 14566390 Royal Electrical and Mechanical Engineers, who died on Sunday, 30th. December, 1945 aged 22.

He was the son of Mr. an Mrs. S. Howe, husband of Kathleen May Howe, of Hayes.

He died of an intestinal obstruction in a Naples hospital and is buried at Naples War Cemetery, Italy. Grave 1V. 0. 6.

HOWELL Frederick James

Gunner 1156363 30 Field Regiment, Royal Artillery, who died on Saturday, 16th. September, 1944 aged 21.

He was the son of Ada Howell, of Hayes.

The 30 Field Regiment was of part of the 4th. Infantry Division who landed in Italy on the 21st. February, 1944 They had taken part in the advance from the south of Italy. He died during the advance from Ancona to Rimini (which broke the *Gothic* Line) and in the heavy fighting around Rimini which was taken by the Allies on the 21st. September, 1944.

He is buried at Gradara War Cemetery, Italy. Grave II. A.11, and commemorated at St. Mary's, Hayes. Gradara is midway between Pesaro and Riccione.

HUCKELL Frederick

Fusilier 6457122 2nd. Battalion, Royal Fusiliers (City of London) Regiment), who died on Friday, 31st. May, 1940 aged 27.

He was the son of Mr. and Mrs. F.W. Huckell, of Cranford, Middx; husband of Mrs. E.L. Huckell, of Harlington.

The 2nd. Battalion was part of the 12th. Brigade of the 4th. Infantry Division who were sent to France in October 1939.   When the Germans attacked in the Ardennes on the 10th. May the British Expeditionary Force advanced into Belgium to head off the Germans as planned beforehand. Belgium never declared war on Germany and only entered when invaded.

The battalion took up defensive positions near Brussels but were forced to withdraw on the 18th. when "the Belgians on their flank withdrew at the first shot and left them exposed." On the 23rd. May they withdrew to west of Nieuport where they fought as the rearguard whilst the BEF was evacuated from Dunkirk.   The Belgians surrendered unconditionally on the 28th. May, without informing their allies.   Frederick died on the 31st. and on the 1st. June, the survivors of the battalion were withdrawn to Dunkirk.   There they boarded the little minesweeper H.M.S. *Speedwell* who took most of the battalion in the 1,500 troops she saved and who reached Dover at 1400 hrs.

He is buried at Oostduinkerke Communal Cemetery, Koksijde, West Vlaanderen, Belgium. Row G. Grave 151, and commemorated at St. Peter's and St. Paul's, Harlington.

HUNT William James
Rifleman 6916723 8th. (2nd Battalion The London Rifle Brigade) Battalion, Rifle Brigade, who died on Thursday, 29th. June, 1944, aged 27.
He was the son of Albert E. and Louisa Hunt; husband of Marion Hunt, of Hayes.
The 6th. Battalion was part of the 11th. Armoured Division who landed in Normandy on the 9th. June, D + 3. and were now engaged in the heavy fighting against the SS units.
Operation *Epsom*, the third attempt to capture Caen was to start on the 26th. June with an outflanking attack to the west of Caen. The attempt to capture the key point, the notorious Hill 112 had failed and 8 RB had withdrawn and were digging in. They were then ordered to retake the hill which they did, but William died in the attack. Unfortunately they were unable to hold the hill against German counter attacks and were forced to withdraw once more.
He is buried at Banneville-La-Campagne, War Cemetery, Calvados, France. Grave X11. D. 7, and commemorated at St. Mary's, Hayes.

HURST Desmond Andrew
Private 14384418 1/6th. Battalion, The Queen's Royal Regiment (West Surrey), who died on Thursday, 3rd. August, 1944 aged 19.
He was the son of Ralph R. and Clementine Hurst, of Hayes.
The 1/6th. Battalion was the part of the Motorised 131st. Infantry Brigade of the 7th. Armoured Division, (The Desert Rats) who had arrived in Normandy on the 10th. June. They were taking part in a six division offensive south of Caen, near Mount Pincon. Desmond died in the heavy fighting. The object of this was to prevent the Germans transferring forces to their left flank as the Americans had just broken through at St. Lo, left the bocage and were now in open country heading for Avranches and eventually Paris, which was surrendered to the French forces on the 25th, the Americans having stood aside to let the French have the honour of liberating their capital.
He is buried at Bayeaux War Cemetery, Calvados France. Grave XXV1. D. 21, and commemorated at St. Mary's, Hayes.

HUTCHINSON Ronald William
Steward C/LX782280 H.M.S. *Vengeance*, Royal Navy, who died on Sunday, 17th. August, 1947 aged 18.
He was the son of Reginald W. and Edith A. Hutchinson, of Woodrow Avenue, Hayes, and was a Officers Steward on the aircraft carrier *Vengeace*.
He died at the Royal Naval Hospital, Haslar, Gosport of poliomyelitis.
He is buried at Hayes and Harlington (Cherry Lane) Cemetery. Sec. C.3. Grave O. 34, and commemorated at St. Mary's, Hayes.

HUTCHINSON W J
Although commemorated at St. Mary's, Hayes, unfortunately I have not been able to trace this person

HUTCHISON J
Although commemorated at St. Mary's, Hayes, unfortunately I have not been able to trace this person

INGLEDOW James Henry Havelock
Gunner 1532125 585 Independent Heavy Anti-Aircraft Battery, Royal Artillery, who died on Saturday, 17th. July, 1943 aged 25.
He was the son of William and Agnes Ingledow; husband of Emily Alice Ingledow, of Hayes. and was living at Cobden Street, Kettering, Northants. In civilian life he was a bricklayers assistant.
He was found drowned twelve miles out at sea off Liverpool but "how he came to be in the water the evidence is insufficient to show" the coroner said at the inquest.
He is buried at Kettering (London Road) Cemetery, Northants. Row 00 Grave 21.

INNS Richard Leslie
Lance Bombardier 958334 72 Anti-Tank Regiment, Royal Artillery, who died on Sunday, 27th. August, 1944 aged 25.
He was the son of Frank and Alice Inns, of Harlington.
The 72nd. Regiment was part of the 6th. Armoured Division which arrived in Italy on the 18th. March, 1944.
The Commonwealth forces which comprised 8th. Army launched Operation *Olive* on the 25th. August, 1944, to advance eastwards from the town of Arezzo on the River Arno in Tuscany, and cross over the Apennines to reach the Adriatic coast at Ancona. The German Commander *Kesselring* had been distracted by Operation *Dragoon*, the landings in Southern France and had moved some of his troops to the French/Italian border to prevent a breakout into Italy.
The Germans were therefore taken by surprise and in four days fell back to the main *Gothic* Line. Richard died in this advance,
He is buried at Arezzo War Cemetery, Italy. Grave V1. E.17, and is commemorated at St. Mary's. Harmondsworth.

JAMES George Richard
Corporal 6699527 1/6th. Battalion, East Surrey Regiment, who died on Tuesday, 28th. May, 1940 aged 35.
He was the son of William and Agnes James; husband of Lilian Winnifred James, of Hayes.
The East Surreys was part of the 10th Brigade of the 4th. Infantry Division who were sent to France in October 1939 to join the British Expeditionary Force.
On the 10th. May the German Blitzkrieg began and they soon reached the coast at Abbeville on the 20th. May. The British were now retreating and thinking seriously of evacuation. James died in the Battle of the Ypres and the Comines canal which took place from the 26th. to the 28th. May. The rest of the army was evacuated from Dunkirk, the last British troops leaving on the 2nd. June.
He is buried at Oostduinkerke Communal Cemetery, Koksijde. West Vlaanderen, Belgium. Row A. Grave 19.

JARVIS A.A..
Although commemorated at St. Mary's, Hayes, unfortunately I have not been able to trace this person

JOHNSON Henry William James
Leading Aircraftman 1181715 R.A.F.V.R. who died on Tuesday, 29th. September, 1942 aged 22.
He was the son of William and Ada Johnson; husband of Kathleen Mary Johnson, of Hayes.
He was serving with 200 Squadron who were flying Hudson 111 a s on anti-submarine duties and was based in Gambia, West Africa. He was admitted to 55 General Hospital on the 27th. September seriously ill with meningitis and died two days later.
He is buried at Fajara War Cemetery, Gambia. Grave 4. F. 8.

JONES Gordon Baden

Sergeant 1892748 R.A.F.V.R. who died on Saturday, 26th. August, 1944 aged 19.

He was the son of John B. and Margaret Jones, of Hayes.

He was Flight Engineer flying Lancaster 1 s with 75 Squadron of 3 Group based at Mepal, Cambs. They took off at 3023 hrs. to attack Russelsheim and were shot down over the target.

All seven crew are buried at Durnbach War Cemetery, Bad Tolz, Bayern, Germany. Gordon's grave is 5. H. 11. He is commemorated at St. Mary's, Hayes.

412 Lancasters were despatched to bomb the Opel Motor works. The Pathfinders were very accurate, the actual raid took only 10 minutes and extensive damage was done, and only 15 aircraft lost. This was Bomber Command at its apogee.

JOYS Reginald Harry

Fusilier 6471365 1st. Battalion, Royal Fusiliers (City of London Regt.), who died on Sunday, 18th. June, 1944 aged 28.

He was the son of Harry and Annie Joys.

The 1st. Battalion was the English Battalion of the 17th. Indian Infantry Brigade of the 4th. Indian Infantry Division who arrived in Italy as part of Eighth Army on the 24th. September, 1943. They took part in the Cassino battles; Rome had fallen on the 5th. June, and the Allies were now ready for the advance northwards.

The American Fifth Army was to advance up the East coast in two columns and the Eighth Army advance in the centre, the object being the capture of Florence and the crossing of the River Po by the second half of July. The Eighth Army encountered their first real opposition between Lake Bolseno and Terni in which fighting Reginald was killed.

He is buried at Assisi War Cemetery. Grave 1V. H. 7, and commemorated at St. Mary's, Hayes.

JUDD Stanley

Sapper 2129763 503 Field Company, Royal Engineers who died on Thursday, 9th. September, 1943 aged 29.

He was the son of Frederick and Winifred Judd; husband of Eileen Judd, of Bootle, Lancs. He was a resident of Middx.

The 503 Company took part in the invasion of Italy, landing on the beaches south of Salerno in the early hours of the 9th. September (Operation Avalanche). The Allies object was to seize Naples, 50 difficult miles to the west.. Based in Sicily the Allied landings had to take place within a radius of 250 miles, which was the range of the Allies main fighter, the Spitfire. Unfortunately the Germans had appreciated this and were ready to rush large forces to Salerno.

Therefore the landings were bitterly contested and Stanley died in the fierce fighting on the first day. By the 17th. the Germans had given up with their attacks, and on the 23rd. Naples fell.

He is commemorated on the Cassino Memorial, Panel 3, and St. Mary's, Hayes.

KEENE Ronald Ernest

Sergeant 1334731 R.A.F.V.R. who died on Friday, 15th. January, 1943 aged 21.

He was the son of George R. and Florence M. Keene, of Hayes.

He was a Wireless Operator / Air Gunner with 16 Operational Training Unit flying Wellington 111 s from Barford St. John, Oxon. They took off to carry out night circuits and landings. At approx.2155 hours an engine cut out which lead to a crash on rising ground about 4 miles east of the airfield, and less than a mile NNE of Aynho, Northants, some 3 miles SSE of Banbury. Both Ronald and the pilot P/O Boodrie were killed.

He is buried at Middleton Stoney (All Saints) Churchyard., Oxon. Plot 2. Row G. Grave 10.

KEEN Harold Frederick
Engineman LT/KX 149138 *H.M.B.Y. Minesweeper 2035*, Royal Naval Patrol Service, who died on
Sunday, 5th. November, 1944 aged 20.
He was the son of Arthur and Dorothy C. Keen, of Harlington.
H.M. Brooklyn Yard Minesweepers were named after the yard where they were designed, and were
made of wood to counter the enemy's use of magnetic mines. She displaced 210 tons, was diesel
powered and had a speed of 13 knots. She was armed with 1 * 3 inch and 2 * 20 mm. guns.
Walcheren was taken by the Canadians and by the 5th. November minesweeping could commence.
His minesweeper was not sunk and he was probably killed by enemy aircraft who straffed the little
boats.
112 Minesweepers were assigned the task of sweeping the Schelde and it was not finally declared
free of mines until November 28th, when the port of Antwerp was opened.
He is buried at Oostende New Communal Cemetery, Oostende, West Vlaanderen, Belgium Plot 9.
Row 7. Grave 1 2, and commemorated at St. Peter's and St. Paul's, Harlington.

Please see note below.

Antwerp and the Scheldt

In September 1944 the Allies missed the great opportunity to overrun both banks of the Scheldt and
open the port of Antwerp, which was fifty miles from the sea. If they had done this they would have
cut off thousands of Germans withdrawing along the coast from France and Belgium to Holland and
Germany. Unfortunately *Montgomery* and the British plans were to take Arnhem and open a route
into the Ruhr, and *Bradley* and the Americans to push into the Saar and reach the Rhine. Both had
failed and now their lines of communication were so long their advances had to be halted. Now in
October Eisenhower gave orders to *Montgomery* to clear the Scheldt.
To open the port of Antwerp meant capturing the islands of South Beveland, North Beveland and
Walcheren, all of which had large dykes and were of reclaimed soil. It was therefore decided that
Bomber Command should destroy the dykes and on the 3rd. October 243 Lancasters attacked them.
So successful was this raid that by the middle of October three quarters of Walcheren was under
water, and the Germans were confined to the towns of Flushing and Middleburg. The assault on
Walkcheren was carried out by amphibious forces from the south and west and by land forces across
the causeway from the east. These attacks were carried out by the Canadians and by the 2nd,
November after two weeks of savage fighting the islands were occupied.

KELLOND Wallace Llewelyn
Craftsman 2047923 21 Beach Recovery Section, Royal Electrical and Mechanical Engineers, who
died on Wednesday, 1st. November, 1944 aged 24.
He was the son of Albert E. and Alice A. Kellond, of Hayes; husband of Eva Kellond, of Wisewood,
Sheffield. He died in the final battles for Walcheren and was lost at sea, He is therefore
commemorated at Groesbeek Memorial, Gelderland, Holland. Panel 9, and at St. Peter's and St.
Paul's, Harlington.

KELLY Ernest George
Lance Corporal 6101584 14th. Battalion, The Queen's Royal Regiment (West Surrey), who died on
Saturday, 21st. December, 1940 aged 25.
He was the son of Mr. and Mrs. T. Kelly, of Hayes.
He was killed when a landmine exploded on the foreshore of Medmerry Beach, Selsey, West Sussex.
He is buried at Gerrards Cross (St. James) Churchyard, Bucks. Grave 564.

KIDD Ernest John

Cook (S) P/MX 64221 H.M. Boom Defence Vessel *Tunisian*, Royal Navy, who died on Thursday, 9th. July, 1942.

Boom Defence Vessels were used to protect harbours from enemy E-Boats, submarines, midget submarines, and frogmen by means of a boom with suspended heavy netting. The *Tunisian* displaced 238 tons and was built in 1930. She hit a mine and sank in the Harwich area.

He is commemorated on the Portsmouth Naval Memorial, Panel 70 Column 1, and St. Mary's, Hayes.

KNOWLES David William

Fusilier 6457078 2nd. Battalion, Royal Fusiliers (City of London Regiment), who died on Monday, 13th. October, 1941 aged 28.

He was the son of George and Mary Knowles; husband of Annie Irene Beatrice Knowles, of Lansbury Drive, Hayes.

He died at the District Hospital, Newbury of "inhalation of carbon monoxide fumes from a fire in an unventilated room when sleeping".

He is buried at Hayes and Harlington (Cherry Lane) Cemetery. Sec. C.1. Grave T.12..

LANDER Henry Granville

Sapper 5445433 276 Field Company, Royal Engineers, who died on Sunday, 5th. November 1944 aged 33.

He was the son of Harry P. and Mary A. Lander; husband of Eva Sarah Lander, of Hayes.

The 276 Field Company was part of the divisional troops of the 51st. Highland Infantry Division and he died in Operation *Guy Fawkes*, at the end of which the General Officer commanding said "We of the Highland Division can look back on the successful operation completed. During the period 23rd. October to the 7th. November HD by its thrust from Scijndel to Gertrudenberg and its activities east and north of s'Hertogenbosch cleared an area of some 300 square miles of Holland, denied the Germans their escape route and captured or annihilated most of their rearguards south of the River Mass.

The operation included assault crossing of two rivers, the forcing of the narrow causeway from Waspik to Gertrudenberg and the assault crossing of the Aftwaterings canal. The casualties of the division amounted to 44 officers, 630 other ranks, of whom 7 officers and 115 ORs were killed. Prisoners captured totalled 30 officers and 2378 ORs and enemy casualties must have been very heavy".

Henry died on what was virtually the last day of the battle.

He is buried at Bergen-op-Zoom War Cemetery, Noord Brabant, Holland. Grave 17. A. 11. Bergen is a town 40 kms. north-east of Antwerp, Belgium. and the cemetery contains 1279 casualties of WW2.

LASCELLES Edwin Herbert

Leading Aircraftman 1222580 6341 Light Warning Unit, R.A.F.V.R who died on Monday, 18th. September, 1944 aged 34.

He was the son of William and Daisy Lascelles; husband of Edith Winifred Lascelles (nee Redfearn) of Hayes.

He was a Wireless Operator and although the CWGC records states he died on the 18th. the RAF records state he died on the last day of the battle, the 25th.

He is buried at Arnhem Oosterbeek War Cemetery, Gelderland, Holland. Grave 4. C. 7, and commemorated at St. Mary's, Hayes.

Please see note after Alexander BAISDEN

LAST Sidney George
Private 5771650 1st. Battalion, Royal Norfolk Regiment, who died on Saturday, 8th. July, 1944 aged 27.
He was the son of George and Annie Last; husband of Phyllis Mary Last, of Hayes.
The 1st. Norfolks was part of the 185th. Brigade of the 3rd. Infantry Division (*Monty's* Ironsides).
They had landed in Normandy on D-Day and had been involved in the heavy fighting since then.
The Canadians had just taken Carpiquet airfield, near Caen and were holding it against fierce German counterattacks.
Now *Montgomery* launched Operation *Charnwood*, his grand slam operation by 1 Corps to finally take Caen. On July 7th. 467 Lancasters and Halifaxes dropped 2,560 tons of bombs on the northern outskirts of Caen. At dawn next morning, greatly heartened by this massive display of air power, 1 Corps, consisting of 3rd. British on the left, 59th.British in the centre, and 3rd. Canadian on the right attacked. These divisions were to converge on the city, clear it and seize crossings over the river Orne. In the centre the opposition from 12th. SS was as firm as ever and the 59th. had to battle for every village. On the left the opposition was low grade and the 3rd. were able to reach the northern outskirts. The following morning (the 8th.) patrols made their way into the centre, and bulldozers attempted to clear the streets. The City of Caen was now in British hands, but Sidney had died achieving that success.
He is buried at La Deliverance War Cemetery, Douvres, Calvados. Grave V11. C. 10.

LAUDER Frederick James
Sergeant 1331489 R.A.F.V.R. who died on Monday, 3rd. May, 1943 aged 22.
He was the son of Harry J. and Dorothy A. Lauder, of Hayes.
He was a Wireless Operator / Air Gunner flying Halifax 11 s with 51 Squadron of 4 Group based at Snaith, Yorks. They took off on a training flight and crashed at 1540 hrs, due to engine failure, at Botany Bay between Barnby Dun and Dunscroft, villages some 5 miles north east of Doncaster. All seven of the crew were killed.
He is buried at Hayes (St. Mary's) Churchyard, Hayes, and is commemorated on the Church Memorial.

LAUDER Gordon William
Flight Sergeant 1865921 R.A.F.V.R. who died on Thursday, 19th. April, 1945
He was a Wireless Operator / Air Gunner with 454 (R.A.A.F) flying Martin Baltimore 111 s based at Gambut, Libya, (Near Bardia). The Baltimore was an American medium day bomber with a top speed of 320 m.p.h., a bomb-load of 2,000 lbs. and a range of 2,800 miles.
The Germans were moving their supplies down by night from the North of Italy and Gordon's Squadron was sent on night intruder patrols. They followed a route Padua, Brescia, Lake Garda and then back to the river Po. Unfortunately he failed to return and Gordon was killed with his other three crew members. They are buried at Padua War Cemetery. Collective Grave V. C 3-6, and George is commemorated at St. Mary's, Hayes.

LAW Albert
Driver T/177730 250 (Airborne) Light Component Company, Royal Army Service Corps, who died on Monday, 25th. September, 1944 aged 25.
He was the husband of Mrs. E. F. Law, of Harlington.
He died on the last day of the Battle of Arnhem trying to escape across the Rhine to the advancing XXX Corps, and is commemorated at Groesbeek Memorial, Gelderland, Holland. Panel 9
Please see the note after Alexander **BAISDEN**

LAWS George Edward
Lance Corporal 6081271 1/6th. Battalion, The Queen's Royal Regiment (West Surrey), who died on Wednesday, 30th. September, 1942 aged 38.
He was the husband of Sarah Laws, of Harlington, Hayes.
At the Battle of Alam Halfa (known as the 1st. Battle of El Alamein) which took place on the 30th. August to the 7th. September, *Montgomery* had decisively beaten *Rommel*. *Monty* had anticipated *Rommel's* right hook to link up with the only road, which ran along the coast and everything that moved was dug in on the Alam Halfa ridge, and this nullified *Rommel's* skill with mobile armour. *Rommel* could now see that this was the beginning of the end for the Axis in Africa, and went on the defensive to prepare for the next and decisive battle. George died in the patrolling before the Battle of El Alamein started on the 25th. October. Please see note on the battle after **J.W. PEACOCK**
He is buried at El Alamein War Cemetery, Egypt. Grave XXV11. B. 21.

LEAKE William Eric
Flight Sergeant 1602731 R.A.F.V.R who died on the 13th. August, 1944 aged 30.
He was the son of Harold and Alice Leake; husband of Bessie Olive Leake, of Southall.
He was a navigator flying Beaufighter X s with 404 (R.C.A.F.) Squadron of Coastal Command based at Strubby, Lincs. They took off on an armed reconnaissance over the Bay of Biscay and were shot down by enemy flak.
He is buried at Le-Bois-Place-En-Re Communal Cemetery Grave 1 and is commemorated at St. Mary's, Hayes. The cemetery is on the Ile de Re, an island off the Biscay coast opposite La Rochelle. As the pilot is not buried in the same cemetery, he could not have ben recovered from the sea.

LEAROYD Philip John
Fusilier 19022175 Royal Fusiliers (City of London Regt.), who died on Thursday, 12th. June, 1947 aged 19.
He was the son of William H. and Kathleen P. Learoyd, of Hayes End.
Although this was nearly two years after the war ended he was killed by an ammunition explosion on a training exercise.
He is buried at Munster Heath War Cemetery, Telgte, Nordrhein-Westfalen, Germany. Grave 1. B. 7.

LENAHAN John Desmond
Pilot Officer 41302 R.A.F. who died on Monday, 9th. September, 1940 aged 20.
He was the son of John M. and Sarah E. Lenahan, of Hayes.
The Battle of Britain was reaching its climax and by September the 8th. the enemy plan seemed clearer now. Bomb London by night and accept some small losses; bomb London by day covered by a big fighter escort which would neutralise the rest of Fighter Command and then invade.
The Luftwaffe launched a 200 bomber raid plus as many or more fighters in the early evening and both 11 and 12 Groups took off to attack them. John was flying Hurricane 1 s with 607 Squadron based at Tangmere. Sussex. He was shot down at 1750 hrs. in an engagement with Do. 17 bombers and Me 109 fighters over Mayfield, East Sussex and crashed at Mount Ephraim, Cranbrook. Two of his colleagues P/O S. B. Parnall and P/O G. J,. Drake also died in this dog-fight but Sgt. R. A. Spyer parachuted to safety. The R. A. F lost 19 aircraft on this day. and the Germans 28. But the German attacks that night resulted in 400 killed and 1400 injured in London.
He is buried at Cranbrook Cemetery, Kent. Sec. O. Grave 58.

LETT Maurice Lewis
Lance Corporal 14426088 5th. Battalion, Black Watch (Royal Highlanders), who died on Sunday, 25th. February, 1945 aged 19.
The 5th. Battalion was part of 27th. Infantry Brigade of the 51st. Highland Infantry Division who landed in Normandy on the 7th. June, D-Day +1. The Highland Division, reformed in 1940 had fought from El Alamein, Libya to the River Sangro in Italy, and had now advanced across France, Belgium, and Holland, to Germany. As he was only 19 he probably joined the Division as a replacement when they returned to the U.K. in early 1944.
The XXX Corps Commander General *Horrocks* (*Montgomery's* favourite General) wrote to the Officer commanding the Highland Division after the battle.
"I have seen 51st. Highland Division fight many battles since I first met them just before Alamein. But I am certain that the Division has never fought better then in the recent offensive into Germany. You breached the enemy's defences in the initial attack, fought your way through the southern part of the Reichswald, overcame in succession several strong points of the Siegfried line such as Hekkens and then finally cleared Goch, a key centre in the German defensive line (where Maurice was killed). You have accomplished everything that you have been asked to do in spite of a number of additional German reserves which have been thrown in at your front. No Division has been asked to do more and no Division has ever accomplished more. Well done, Highland Division."
He is buried at the Rheinberg War Cemetery. Kamp Lintfort, Nordrhein-Westfal, Germany Grave 12. E. 18. and commemorated at St. Mary's, Hayes.

LEWIS Ivor Wells
Bombardier 808595 135 (The Hertfordshire Yeomanry) Field Regiment, Royal Artillery, who died on Wednesday,11 February, 1942 aged 27.
He was the son of Albert E, and Elizabeth Lewis; husband of Betsy Mary Mira Lewis, of Hayes. They were the divisional artillery of the 18th. Infantry Division who were originally bound for the Middle East but diverted to Bombay when Japan invaded Malaya and then sent to Singapore, arriving on the 29th. January. They were then sent into the final battle for Singapore and Ivor died four days before the Allied surrender.
Please see note after Gerald **GREEN**
He is commemorated at Kranji War Cemetery, Singapore. Special Memorial 31. A. 9. and at St. Albans Cathedral.

LOFTUS Terence William Peter
Rifleman 6853611 2nd. Battalion, King's Royal Rifle Corps, who died on Monday, 10th. July, 1944 aged 19.
He was the son of Edward and Eileen M. Loftus, of Hayes.
The 2nd. Battalion was part of the 4th. Armoured Brigade who arrived in Normandy on D+1, the 7th. June. They were attached to the British 8 Corps.
For details of his death please see entry after **Kenneth BEEBE**.
He is buried at St. Manvieu War Cemetery, Cheux, Calvados, France. Grave V111. H. 15.and commemorated at St. Mary's Hayes.

LYDON John Patrick
Gunner 1128888 139 Field Regiment, Royal Artillery, who died on Sunday, 6th. February, 1944 aged 42.
He was the son of Michel and Margaret Ellen Lydon; husband of Phyllis Muriel Lydon, of Yiewsley 139 Field Regiment arrived in India in October 1942 and were moved to the Arakan front in September 1943. As part of the 5th. and 7th. Indian Divisions they advanced astride the Mayu

range. He died in the fierce fighting that ensued which resulted in the first reversal the Japanese suffered in Burma. He was moved from his original resting place in 1951 to ensure that his grave received the care and attention it deserved.
He is buried at Taukkyan War Cemetery, Burma (now Myanmar). Grave 5. G. 16. and commemorated at St. Mary's, Hayes.

McDIARMID Eric Aubrey
Stoker 1st. Class D/KX 164350 H.M.S. *Lothian*, Royal Navy, who died on Friday, 6th. April, 1945 aged 34.
He was the son of Samuel J. and Sarah A. McDiarmid; husband of Isabel McDiarmid, of Hayes. Despite this researcher's best endeavours it has not been possible to trace this vessel. But he was definitely lost at sea and is commemorated on the Plymouth Naval Memorial, Panel 94, Column 3, and at St. Mary's, Hayes.

McENTEGART John
Lance Sergeant 3651386 1st. Battalion, South Lancashire Regiment, who died on Tuesday 6th. June, 1944 aged 33.
He was the son of Lydia McEntegart and stepson of Herbert Riley; husband of Margaret McEntegart (nee Hooker), of Hayes.
The 1st. Battalion was part of the 8th. Brigade of the 3rd. British Infantry Division. known affectionately as "*Monty's Ironsides*". After reaching England after Dunkirk they spent the next four years training for the return to the continent in the invasion of Normandy. They were loaded over the sides of the transport ships between 0430 and 0500 on June 6th. Their target was Queen Red Beach of Sword Beach. By nightfall they had captured Hermanville, 13 kms. north of Caen and secured the beach-head, ready for the follow-up troops. That day the battalion had lost 18 officers and men killed in action, one of whom was John. They had also eighty-nine wounded, and nineteen missing. Their objective of capturing Caen on the first day was not possible, because they never landed enough tanks to go on the offensive against 21st. Panzer, who might even have been reinforced by 12th. SS Panzer.
He is buried at Hermanville War Cemetery, Calvados France. Grave 1. J. 13.
Also buried here is John **PERRIN**, of the same regiment and Cowley, Uxbridge, who also died on D-Day.

MACKRODT Archibald Vernon
Captain, Royal Indian Service Corps, who died on Monday, 18th. May, 1942.
He was the son of Mr. and Mrs. G. MacKrodt; husband of B. MacKrodt, of Hayes.
He died in the long retreat from Burma into India in early 1942. (Please see Ronald **Hipsey**). The main retreating forces had reached India on the 15th, and Archibald probably died as one of the many stragglers who could not get across the river Chindwin and on to India,.
He is commemorated on The Rangoon Memorial, Burma (Myanmar). Face.75.

McMAHON David
Sergeant 7928018 2nd. Fife and Forfar Yeomanry, Royal Armoured Corps, who died on Friday, 22nd. September, 1944 aged 36.
He was the son of David and Margaret McMahon; husband of Gladys Martha McMahon, of Hayes. The 2nd. Fife and Forfar Yeomanry, armed with Sherman tanks was the reconnaissance squadron of the 11th. Armoured Division which was known as the Black Bull division because of their emblem. They had landed in Normandy on the 23rd. June. Not directly involved in the Battle of Arnhem they were 85 miles to the south and as part of V111 Corps were keeping up the pressure on the Germans.

They crossed the Escaut canal near Venlo and were proceeding northwards on the left bank of the river Mass. David was in command of a Sherman tank and died fighting in this difficult watery terrain, where every bridge was vital.

He is buried at Mierlo War Cemetery, Noord-Brabant, Holland. Grave V. A. 13.

Please see note after Alexander **BAISDEN**

McNAMARA Edward Cowndon

Leading Seaman C/JX 147884 H.M.S. *Duchess*, Royal Navy, who died on Tuesday, 12th. December, 1939 aged 28.

He was the son of Thomas and Ellen A. McNamara, of Hayes.

The *Duchess* was a destroyer of 1375 tons built in 1932, armed with four 4.7 inch guns and eight torpedo tubes. She was sunk when she collided with the battleship *Barham* (30,000 tons and sank in the Mediterranean in 1941) in the North Channel, West Coast of Scotland. Six officers, and 123 ratings including Edward were lost. One officer and 22 ratings were picked up.

He is commemorated on the Chatham Naval Memorial. Panel 33.1.

McNAMARA Ronald

Sergeant 915420 R.A.F.V.R. who died on Tuesday, 14th. October, 1941.

He was a Wireless Operator / Air-gunner with 22 Operational Training Unit flying Wellington 1 C s from Wellesbourne Mountford, Warwickshire.

They took off on a navigational exercise, and encountered poor weather conditions whilst flying in cloud, lost control and dived into the ground at 1044 hrs. not far from the Gloucestershire-Oxon. border, about a mile west of Cornwell, 3 miles west of Chipping Norton. All five members of the crew including Ronald were killed. The two Canadian members were buried at Little Rissington and the other three were returned home.

He is buried at Cranford (St. Dunstan) Churchyard, Cranford, Middx, and commemorated at St. Peter's and St. Paul's, Harlington.

MAKIN George

Private 4122945 2nd Battalion, Cheshire Regiment, who died on Saturday, 17th. June, 1944 aged 32.

He was the son of Thomas and Helen Makin; husband of Rose Elizabeth Makin, of Hayes.

The 2nd Cheshires was the Machine Gun Battalion of the 50th. (Northumberland) Division who landed in Normandy on the 6th. June, D-Day. (Please see Richard **HALL** of Harlington who served in this division and who died on June 14th).

George died in the continuing efforts to tie down the German forces opposing the British and Canadian positions and prevent them being moved to oppose the Americans. This was becoming very successful. By the 20th. *Montgomery* now had twenty divisions ashore, and *Rommel* only eighteen in Normandy, due to Operation "*Bodyguard*" the deception plan which convinced *Hitler* that the real invasion would take place in the Pas de Calais, and the Normandy landings were a diversion. As *Rommel* said "I am not able to attack, all I can do is tie a noose around the bridgehead".

He is buried at Bayeux War Cemetery, Calvados, France. Grave X1V. H. 13.

MALLETT Ronald Spencer DFC

Flying Officer 158594 R.A.F.V.R. who died on the Wednesday, 28th. June, 1944.

He was a navigator flying Mosquito 11 s with 141 Squadron of 8 Group based at West Raynham, Norfolk.

They took off at 2310 hrs. for a patrol over Northern France, using the *Serrate* device to home in on the emissions from the German night-fighter's radar. But they themselves were attacked over

Holland by a night-fighter and exploded, throwing clear the pilot F/L Engelbach. Debris from the Mosquito was found near Weert (Limburg) and Ronald was taken for burial at Eindhoven (Woensel) General Cemetery. Plot KK. Grave 99. He is commemorated at St. Mary's Hayes.
RONALD was awarded the Distinguished Flying Cross on the 9th. June, 1944.when he was serving with the same Squadron.

The citation in the London Gazette states,
"This Officer has completed a very large number of sorties and his record is worthy of the greatest praise. He is an extremely efficient and determined member of aircraft crew and has assisted in the destruction of two enemy aircraft at night".

MALPAS Alfred Charles
Gunner 11428274 6/3 Maritime Regiment, Royal Artillery, who died on Saturday. 7th. November, 1942 aged 31.
He was the son of David W. and Anne Malpas; husband of Jennie Malpas, of Hayes.
It has not been able to trace the exact ship he went down with. There are four alternatives.

1. S.S. *Roxby* torpedoed and sunk by U.613
2. S.S. *Glenlea* torpedoed and sunk by U.566
3. S.S. *D'Entrecasteaux* torpedoed and sunk by U.154
4. S.S. *Lindenhall* torpedoed and sunk by U 506

All these vessels were lost on the 7th. November and all were of sufficient size to mount a gun and have a gunnery crew aboard. Six members of the Royal Artillery died that day at sea.
He is commemorated on the Chatham Naval Memorial. Panel 67.2.

MANSFIELD Norman Leonard
Telegraphist D/SSX 30203 H.M.S. *Sultan*, Royal Navy, who died on Monday, 16th, February, 1942 aged 20.
He was the son of Leonard H. and Florence Mansfield, of Hayes.
H.M.S. *Sultan* was not a ship but the Royal Naval base at Singapore. Having advanced down through Malaya the Japanese had now crossed the causeway on to the island of Singapore, and on the 14th. February there was fighting in the streets of the city.
General *Percival* surrendered the Allied forces on the 15th. and all fighting ceased at 20.30 hrs. The records states that Norman died on shore, on the day after the ceasefire, how it is not known. But as his grave is also not known he is commemorated on the Plymouth Naval Memorial. Panel 101. Column 3. and at St. Mary's, Hayes.

MARTIN F
Although commemorated at St. Peter's and St. Paul's Harlington, unfortunately I have not been able to trace this person.

MASON Arthur James Cedric
Flight Sergeant 1376810 R.A.F.V.R. who died on Tuesday, 16th. February, 1943 aged 30.
He was the son of Charles and Ethel Mason, of Hayes.
He was an Air Gunner flying Lancaster 1 s with 103 Squadron of 1 Group based at Elsham Wolds. Lincs. They took off at 1859 hrs. to bomb Lorient, the submarine base in Brittany. They crashed in the target area and all seven of them died and are buried at Guidel Communal Cemetery, Morbihan. His grave is Row 5. No. 11

377 aircraft were despatched that night and Arthur's was the only one lost. This was the last of eight raids and left the Lorient base deserted and ruined.

MASON Ronald
Aircraftman 2nd. Class 1628951 R.A.F.V.R.. who died on Saturday, 24th. October, 1942 aged 18. He was the son of Frank K. and Louisa Mason, of Hayes.
Ronald was attached to 11 Recruits Centre, Skegness, Lincs. on general duties. This was the Butlin's Holiday Camp which had been requisitioned by the Government. He was killed when Skegness was bombed at approximately 2142 hrs. The East coast did not present a target of very high priority, but because the Germans were able to locate the targets easily, was frequently attacked, which resulted in Hull being the most bombed British city.
He is buried at Havelock Cemetery, Southall. Grave 1265

MATTHEW John Proven
Lieut-Commander (Engineering) *H.M.S. Mersey* Royal Naval Reserve, who died on Tuesday, 28th. July, 1942 aged 52.
He was the son of William and Elizabeth Matthew; husband of Daphne Dorothy Gladys Matthew, of Longmead Road, Hayes.
H.M.S. Mersey was not a vessel but the No. 6 Depot at Liverpool. He died of cancer at Mount Vernon Hospital, Northwood.
He is buried at Hanwell Cemetery, Middx. Plot 17. Grave 8921

MATTHEWS James Richard George
Flight Sergeant 1287638 R.A.F.V.R.. who died on Monday, 20th. December, 1943.
He was a Wireless Operator / Air Gunner flying Halifax 111 s with 466 (R.A.A.F.) Squadron of 2 Group based at Leconfield, Yorks. They took off at 1704 hrs. to attack Frankfurt and crashed in the vicinity of Wiesbaden. All the crew of seven were killed and rest in the Rheinberg War Cemetery, Collective grave 18. E. 19-25. Rheinberg is 24 kms. north of Krefeld and 13 kms. south of Wesel and was chosen in 1946 as the cemetery to rebury all Commonwealth casualties from the Ruhr and surrounding area. He is commemorated at St. Mary's, Hayes.
650 aircraft were sent to attack this target, and the German controllers were able to plot the Bomber force as it left the English coast and track it all the way to Frankfurt. The diversionary attack on Mannheim was not successful and 41 aircraft of the main force were lost. The raid was not a complete success, but considerable damage was done.

MAXFIELD Frederick
Pilot Officer 132996 R.A.F.V.R. who died on Thursday, 15th. October, 1942 aged 29.
He was the son of Frederick and Margaret Maxwell; husband of Sybil Maxfield, of Hayes.
He was a Wireless Operator / Air Gunner flying Wellington 111 s with 150 Squadron of 1 Group based at Snaith Yorks. They took off to bomb Cologne but were shot down by a night fighter over Holland. All the crew of six including Frederick were killed. He is buried at Ulrum General Cemetery, De Marne, Groningen, Holland. G/H Grave B
289 aircraft were despatched and 18 failed to return to base. This was not a very successful raid as the target was obscured by cloud, and Bomber Command's radio aids (Gee. Oboe) had not yet reached the high standards they did later in the war.

MAYHEW Norman Kenneth
Able Seaman P/JX 243189 H.M.S. *Eclipse*, Royal Navy, who died on Sunday, 24th. October, 1943 aged 20.
He was the son of Stanley C. and Violet R. Mayhew, of Hayes.
H.M.S. *Eclipse* was an E Class destroyer built in 1934, of 1500 tons displacement, with 5 * 4.7 inch guns. The British without the approval or help of the Americans were trying to capture the Dodecanese Islands and open a route through to Istanbul, thus persuading the Turks to join the Allies in the fight against Germany. *Churchill* thought that this was possible with the surrender of Italy, but because the Americans were against the plan, not enough material effort and troops were allocated to it.
She was mined and sank off east of Kalimno, Dodecanese. 119 of her crew including Norman were killed, and 140 of the 200 troops she was transporting also died.
He was commemorated on Portsmouth Naval Memorial. Panel 75. Column 2.

MEABY Ernest Peter
Stoker 1st. Class P/KX 139099 *H.M.L.C.T. 839*, Royal Navy, who died on Wednesday, 2nd. November, 1944.
Landing Craft Tanks were used for taking tanks into action on the invasion beaches. They were of 200 tons displacement and had a speed of 10 knots. No. 839 was taking part in Operation *Infatuate*, the attempt to overrun Walcheren island and particularly the town of Flushing, on which a full amphibious assault was made on the 2nd. Ernest' s ship was sunk but his body was recovered from the sea. Nine craft had been sunk including L.C.T. s 789. and 1133, and 3 Landing Craft Ship (Large) Nos. 252, 256, and 258.
He is buried at Oostende New Communal Cemetery, Belgium, Plot 9. Row 6. Grave 35.and commemorated at St. Mary's, Hayes.
Pleas see note before **Wallace KELLOND**

MELVILLE Alexander
Private 5882267 2nd. Battalion, Northamptonshire Regiment, who died on Thursday, 23rd. May, 1940 aged 28.
He was the son of John and Jean Melville, of Hayes.
The 2nd Battalion was part of the 17th. Brigade of the 5th. Infantry Division who were sent to France to join the British Expeditionary Force in December, 1939.
On May 10th. the Germans broke through the Ardennes, crossed the river Meuse and raced through Belgium and France. They reached the coast on May 20th and cut the Allied forces into two. He died in the defence of Arras, before the decision was made by Lord *Gort*, Commander-in Chief, for the BEF to evacuate through the port of Dunkirk, *Alanbrooke* then commanding 11 Corps, wrote in his diary "Nothing but a miracle can save the BEF". The miracle happened.
He is buried at Maroeuil Communal Cemetery, Pas de Calais. Grave 36.

MICKLEWRIGHT Frederic Henry
Civilian aged 34, who died on Wednesday, 19th. February, 1944 aged 34.
He was the son of Emily Micklewright, of 168, Central Avenue, Hayes; husband of Florence Rosie Micklewright, of 58 Drenon Square, Hayes.
He is commemorated at St. Mary's, Hayes.
For the full details of this incident see entry for Charles **DEAMER**.

MILLS William David

Flight Sergeant 655255 R.A.F. who died on Thursday, 27th. May, 1943 aged 23.
He was the son of David and Jessie Mills; husband of Gladys Joan Mills, of Hayes.
He was a pilot flying Stirling 1 s with 218 (Gold Coast) Squadron of 3 Group based at Downham Market, Norfolk. They took off at 2252 hrs. to carry out a *gardening* operation (mine-laying) in the Friesian Islands, and the were lost without trace. They were the only Stirling lost that night and the crew of seven (average age 22) are commemorated on the Runnymede Memorial, Panel 138. This was the crew's first operational sortie. William is also commemorated at St. Mary's, Hayes.
A reliable source in Holland indicates that the Stirling was shot down by a night-fighter piloted by Ofw Karl-George Pfeiffer from IV. NJG who was operating some 70 kms. off Terschelling. This was a minor minelaying operation in which 23 aircraft took part..

MITTELL Peter

Sub-Lieutenant (Air) H.M.S. *Heron*, R.N.V.R. who died on Sunday, 23rd. March,, 1941 aged 21.
He was the son of Brenchley E. G. and Muriel Mittel, of Jordans Village, Bucks.
H.M.S. *Heron* is the Fleet Air Arm Base at Yeovilton, Somerset (where the F.A.A. Museum is now located). He was serving with 759 Squadron and was flying Gloster Gladiators, the last single engined Biplane fighter used by the R.A.F. and Royal Navy. After completing an air firing exercise he crashed on a hillside at Portwalls Farm, one mile east of Camelford.
He is buried at St. Columb Major Cemetery, Cornwall Grave 305, and commemorated at St. Mary's, Hayes. The R.A.F. base at St.Eval (Coastal Command) is about seven kms. away and this cemetery contains 38 WW2 casualties. one of whom is a German airman.

MOORE Richard Harold

Warrant Officer Class 1 1054683 Regimental Sergeant Major, 63 (The Queen's Own Oxfordshire Hussars) Anti-Tank Regiment, Royal Artillery, who died on Saturday, 11th. May, 1940 aged 36.
He was the husband of Florence Irene Gladys Moore, of Kinmore Crescent, Frogmore Park, Hayes.
He was involved in an accident and was hit by a car in Kineton Road, Wellesbourne. Warwicks, and died from his injuries.
He is buried at Fulham New Cemetery, Surrey. Sec. U.C. Grave 484.

MORRIS Frank Alfred

Serjeant 5571738 5th. Battalion, Wiltshire Regiment, who died on Saturday, 22nd. July, 1944 aged 25.
He was the son of Charles and Ellen Morris, of Harlington; husband of Edith Mary Morris, also of Harlington.
The 5th. Wiltshire with the 4th.Wiltshires and the 4th. Somersets formed the 129th. Brigade of the 43rd. (Wessex) Infantry Division who landed in Normandy on the 23rd. June. He died in the fierce fighting clearing the villages to the north of the Bourguebus ridge during Operation *Goodwood.*
(Please see note after Joseph **NORTON** for the full details)
He is buried at Banneville-La-Campagne War Cemetery, Calvados. Grave X. A. 9, and commemorated at St. Peter's and St. Paul's, Harlington.

MORRIS William Edward

Second Lieutenant 336180 General List, who died on Monday, 9th. October, 1944 aged 31.
He was the son of William and Clara E. Morris; husband of Isabel Margery Morris. of Hayes.
He died of typhoid fever and is buried at Heliopolis War Cemetery, Cairo, Egypt. Grave 6. M. 14.

MORTON Eric
Warrant Officer Class 11 6202896 Battery Sergeant Major. 119 Light Anti-Aircraft Regiment, Royal Artillery, who died on Monday, 19th. February,1945 aged 29.
He was the son of Harry and Norah Morton; husband of Irene Edna Morton of Hayes.
The 119 Light A.A. Regiment was part of the divisional troops of the 15th. Scottish Infantry Division which had landed in Normandy on the 14th. June, 1944 (D-Day +6). They had then taken part in the battles which led to the liberation of France, Belgium, Luxembourg and part of Holland. He died in the battle of the Rhineland which took place between the 8th. February to the 10th. March. The crossing of the Rhine followed and the surrender of the German forces in the West in early May.
He is buried at Groesbeek Canadian War Cemetery, Gelderland, Holland. Grave X11. B. 16, and commemorated at St. Mary's, Hayes, and St. Peter's and St. Paul's, Harlington.

MORTON E.L.
Although commemorated at St. Mary's, Hayes, unfortunately I have not been able to trace this person

MOUDON Cyril Jules
Firewatcher, who died on Tuesday 14th. March 1944 aged 45.
Husband of Emily Elizabeth Moudon, of 33, Crowland Avenue, Harlington He was killed at 33, Crowland Avenue in an air raid.
He is commemorated at St. Mary's, Hayes, and St. Peter's and St. Paul's, Harlington.

MULLEN Mathew
Company Quartermaster Serjeant, 13018179 Pioneer Corps, who died on Wednesday, 22nd. May, 1940 aged 49.
He was the husband of Agatha A. Mullen, of Hayes, formerly of Wills Crescent, Whitton Park, Hounslow, Middx.
He died of a duodenal ulcer at the General Hospital, Southend on Sea.
He is buried at Southend-on-Sea (Sutton Road) Cemetery, Essex. Plot R. Grave 2188.

MURRAY James Lomas
Sergeant 1890416 R.A.F.V.R. who died on Saturday, 4th. August, 1945.
He was serving as a pilot with 13 Operational Training Unit based at Bicester, Oxon., and was flying Mosquito Mk. V1 s. He was involved in a flying accident crashing 1/2 mile off-shore from Filey, East Yorks
He is commemorated on the Runnymede Memorial, Panel 276, St. Mary's, Hayes. and St. Peter's and St. Paul's Harlington. It is interesting to see that he is commemorated on the Runnymede Memorial because the war in Europe had ended in May 1945. But it should be noted that the Commonwealth War Graves Commission Register records all servicemen who died until 1948.

NASH Charles Alfred Richard
Private 6466319 4th. Battalion, Somerset Light Infantry, who died on Sunday, 30th. July, 1944 aged 26.
He was the son of Alfred and Elizabeth Nash, of Hayes.
The 4th. Somersets was part of the 129th. Brigade of the 43rd. Wessex Infantry Division who landed in Normandy on the 23rd. June.
On the Allies right flank facing the weaker part of the German army in Normandy the American in Operation *Cobra* had made the great breakout from Normandy on the 27th. July. They had taken Countances and were advancing on Avranches. It was now vital that *Montgomery* kept up the

pressure to prevent the Germans switching their troops to the front opposite the Americans. He then launched a six division attack southwards and Charles died in the fighting when the 43rd. Division succeeded in capturing Mount Pincon, the highest point in Normandy.

He is buried at Hottot-Les-Bagues War Cemetery, Calvados. Grave V111. F. 4, and commemorated at St. Mary's, Hayes.

NASH George William
Leading Seaman C/J 80658 H.M.S. *Danube 111*, Royal Navy, who died on Sunday, 13th. October, 1940 aged 38.

He was the son of Alfred and Minnie Nash; husband of Mabel Nash, of Hayes.

H.M.S. *Danube 111* was a tug of 234 tons displacement built in 1924 and requisitioned by the Admiralty from its owners. She hit a mine off Sheerness, Kent and sank. The mine was probably one of new magnetic types dropped by German aircraft in the Thames Estuary. The first magnetic mine was disabled in the Thames Estuary in 1940 using copper tools.

He is commemorated on the Chatham Naval Memorial, Panel 34. 3.

NEWTON Albert John   DFM
Flying Officer 53834 R.A.F. who died on Thursday, 4th. May, 1944 aged 29.

He was the husband of D. F. Newton of Hayes.

He was Rear Gunner with 101 Squadron of 1 Group based at Conningsby, Lincs. flying Lancaster 1 s

They took off at 2159 hrs. to bomb the camp at Mailly-Le-Camp. With D-Day only a month away Bomber Command was set the target of attacking this large military camp which was halfway between Rheims and Troyes. They were shot down by a night-fighter, crashing 0200hrs. some 3 kms. SW of Alainville (Seine-et-Oise). All seven crew were killed and are buried at St. Desir War Cemetery, Calvados. Albert's grave is VIII. B.11. This was a successful but very expensive operation. 360 aircraft were sent but 42 were lost, 406 Squadron losing five of their seventeen Lancasters sent.

Ronald D. Wilson DFM. a navigator, of Bishopshalt School and Uxbridge, also died in this raid.

Albert was awarded the Distinguished Flying Medal on the 18th. August, 1941, when he had been serving with No 44 (Rhodesia) Squadron.

The citation in the London Gazette states,

"This airman was a rear gunner in an aircraft which carried out an attack on Essen in daylight. While flying over the Dutch coast this aircraft was intercepted by two enemy fighters. The enemy made successive attacks from the stern. During the third attack Sergeant Newton who had vigorously defended his aircraft throughout was wounded in the feet.

Despite this he continued to engage the enemy and following an accurate burst from his guns, one of the fighters went into a steep dive and was not seen again. The remaining fighter closed for another attack but Sergeant Newton, though in considerable pain met it with absolute power. The attacker broke away and terminated the engagement. By his courage and devotion to duty this airman contributed materially to the safe return of this aircraft".

NORMAN Joseph Henry
Private 4040868 2nd. Battalion, King's Shropshire Light Infantry, who died on Saturday, 22nd. July, 1944 aged 24.

He was the son of Joseph and Margaret Norman, of Hayes End.

The 2nd. Battalion was part of the 185th. Brigade of the 3rd. Infantry Division ("Monty's Ironsides"). They had landed in Normandy on D. Day. They lost 12 officers and 140 other Ranks including Joseph that day. Please see note below.

59

He is buried at La Deliverance War Cemetery, Douvres, Calvados. Grave V1 1 1. E. 4, .and commemorated at St. Mary's, Hayes.

OPERATION GOODWOOD

The plan was for three armoured divisions, the 7th. 11th. and Guards to advance from the Orne bridgehead to the east of Caen and thrust due south. To obtain bomber support *Montgomery* gave a more optimistic version of the outcome than he should have done. Although the bombing was very efficient they were not enough planes to bomb the Bourguebus Ridge which was heavily defended and out of artillery range.

Hitler still believed there would be another landing and was determined to prevent a breakout at Caen, and was moving all available troops into the area. The attack started on the 18th, with the heaviest air attack in support of ground forces ever attempted. But the defences were very deep, line and line of well entrenched positions, and the 11th Armoured had lost half its tanks (125) at the end of the first day, but the infantry (including the 3rd. Division with Joseph) was clearing the German held villages on the north of the ridge.

Operation *Goodwood* ground to a halt; the loss of tanks making it too expensive to continue. *Montgomery* was pleased with the result as it had drawn all the SS Panzers on to the Allied left flank which would allow the American to break out on the right flank at St. Lo. On the 25th. there were seven Panzer divisions opposite the British and Canadians and only one opposite the Americans. Unfortunately *Eisenhower* and the others at SHAEF (Supreme Headquarters Allied Expeditionary Force) did not appreciate *Montgomery*'s battle plan and were furious.

Please note most operations of the British and Canadians in Normandy were named after race-courses.

NUGENT Ronald Harold

Leading Aircraftman 537353 R.A.F. who died on Tuesday, 14th. May, 1940 aged 35.
He was the son of John N. and Florence H. Nugent, of Hayes End.
He was an Wireless Operator flying Battle 1 s with 142 Squadron of the Advanced Air Striking Force based at Berry-au-Bac, near Rheims. The Battle made by Faireys at Hayes, was a single engined light bomber about the size of a Spitfire, with a crew of three, and was virtually obsolete by 1940, being underpowered, too slow and lightly armoured.
The Germans launched their offensive on May 10th. through the Ardennes and 142 Squadron were sent to bomb the German columns. They were hit by ground fire and crashed near Longuyon. All three of them returned safely by truck to their base. The Germans had now crossed the river Meuse and on the 14th. the Squadron were sent to destroy the pontoon bridges. Again they were hit by ground fire and crashed. But this time Ronald and the navigator Sgt. Brookes were killed, but the pilot Sgt. Spear survived. "It was a day calling for raw courage and those that flew into the cauldron at Sedan displayed a determination that won the respect of friend and foe alike". The French compared it to the charge of the Light Brigade ("C'est magnifigue, mais ce n'est pas la guerre.") Note it was not until later in 1940 that all aircrew were promoted to non-commissioned officers. He is buried with the navigator, Sgt. J. Brookes at Choloy War Cemetery, Meurthe-et-Moselle, France. 2A. A. Joint Grave 6.

OAKE James Arthur

Serjeant 6850911 2nd. Battalion, King's Royal Rifle Corps, who died on Sunday, 25th. May, 1947 aged 33.
He was the son of Percy and Ada Oake, of Berwick Avenue, Hayes, and the brother of Stanley, detailed below.

He died of polio at Harefield County Hospital, Harefield, and is buried at Hanwell Cemetery. Plot 4 Grave 9728.

OAKE Stanley
Chief Petty Officer C/J 1108403 H.M.S. *Redmill*, Royal Navy, who died on Friday, 27th. April, 1945 aged 37.
He was the brother of James; husband of Doris May Oake, of Rainham, Kent.
H.M.S. *Redmill* was a *Captain* Class Frigate of 1,300 tons named after Captain Robert Redmill who commanded the *Polyphemus* at Trafalgar. The *Redmill* was torpedoed by U 1105 west of Ireland, 26 miles form Blacksand Bay. Her stern and propeller shafts were blown off and she was towed to Londonderry. Twenty two men including Stanley were killed. She was never repaired and was returned to the U.S.A., after the war. Stanley was buried at sea and is commemorated on the Chatham Naval Memorial. Panel 80.2.

OGDEN Frank Arthur Thomas
Gunner 1128309 92 Field Regiment, Royal Artillery, who died on Saturday 7th. August, 1943 aged 34.
He was the son of James and Elizabeth Ogden, husband of Violet Nithsdale Ogden, of Preston Capes, Northants.
The 92 Field Regiment was now part of the divisional artillery of the 5th. Infantry Division, and had been stationed in Syria and Egypt from May, 1942. The Allies invaded Sicily on the 9th. July, 1942 and Frank landed with his division on the 10th. Frank died in the final battles on the island; the Germans deciding to withdraw to Italy on the 5th. August, crossing the Straits of Messina on the 16th. *Mussolini* had fallen from power on the 25th. July, and had been taken prisoner by the new Italian government.
He is buried at Catania War Cemetery, Sicily, Grave IV. D. 42, and is commemorated at St. Mary's, Hayes.

O'SHEA Maurice
Fusilier 6465162 Royal Fusiliers (City of London) Regiment), who died on Monday, 12th. May, 1947 aged 28.
He was the son of Martin and Kathleen O'Shea; husband of Dorothy Maud O'Shea, of 113 Cleave Avenue, Harlington.
He died of pulmonary tuberculosis at Cleave Avenue. He had been demobilised and was working as an Engineer's Driller.
He is buried at Hayes and Harlington (Cherry Lane) Cemetery. Sec R.1. Grave S. 11, and commemorated at St. Mary's, Hayes.

OTTER Frederick Arthur
Guardsman 2612438 5th. Battalion, Grenadier Guards, who died on Thursday, 27th. January, 1944 aged 31.
He was the son of James and Alice Otter; husband of Elizabeth Caroline Otter, of Hayes.
Please see note after Thomas **CLARE**.
The 5th. Battalion with the 2nd. Coldstream and 1st. Scots. formed the 24th. Guards Infantry Brigade of the 1st. Infantry Division. The Allies had landed at Anzio on the 22nd. and Frederick died in the early fighting trying to expand the beachhead.
He is buried at Anzio War Cemetery, Italy. Grave IV. F. 3.

OXLEY Stanley John
Aircraftman 1st. Class R.A.F. who died on Saturday 13th. September, 1941 aged 19.
He was the son of John. V. and Florence E. Oxley, of Hayes.
He was a Wireless Operator with 8 Squadron, who were flying Blenheim 1V s (twin engine light bombers) from Khormaskar. Aden. He should have been a sergeant because all aircrew were made non-commissioned officers from July 1940. This day he was flying in a Vickers Vincent, which was a two seater army co-operation biplane which was virtually obsolete in 1941. There was an accident and Stanley and the pilot were both killed.. Kindly note Victor **Sennett**, of Ruislip died with this Squadron in July, 1942 bombing Djibouti in a Blenheim.
He is buried at Maala Cemetery, Yemen. Grave H. 49, and commemorated at St. Mary's, Hayes.

PAGE Alexander James
Guardsman 2618275 6th. Battalion, Grenadier Guards, who died on Thursday, 30th. January, 1944 aged 24.
He was the husband of Brenda May Page, of Hayes.
The 6th. Battalion was part of the 22nd. Guards Brigade of the 5th. Infantry Division who had landed at Salerno on the 9th. September, 1943, captured Naples, took part in the crossing of the river Volturno, and in the early battles against the *Gustav* Lime, which ran completely across Italy, through Monte Cassino.
They were now taking part in the advance on the West coast, up Route 7 from Capua to Rome, and crossing the Carigliano near Minturno, which was the eastern end of the *Gustav* Line. The attack began on the 11th. January and the river Carigliano was crossed on the 17th. and the building of bridges began. But the Germans counter-attacked, the Allies were forced to withdraw and Charles died in this heavy fighting.
The advance did not recommence until May, 1944, when the *Gustav* line was breached at Monte Cassino, and the drive to Rome began.
He is buried at Minturno War Cemetery, Italy. Grave 1V. B. 25.

PARISH John Edward
Leading Aircraftman 9817250 R.A.F.V.R. aged 27 who died on Monday, 19th. August, 1940
He was the son of Geoffrey F. and Ada Parish; husband of Ada Parish, of Bury St. Edmunds, Suffolk.
He was stationed at R.A.F. Honington, Suffolk, which was the base for No. 3. Group's 311 Squadron (Wellingtons 1C) and 103 and 105 Squadrons (Fairey Battles), which had just returned from France. John lost his life when the Station was attacked by enemy bombers.
He is buried at Honington (All Saints) Churchyard, Suffolk. Row A. Grave 11, and commemorated at St. Mary's, Hayes, and St. Peter's and St. Paul's, Harlington

PARKER Leslie George
Lance Serjeant 1745617, 393 (The Hampshire Yeomanry) Battery, 72 Heavy Anti-Aircraft Regiment, Royal Artillery, who died on Saturday, 19th. June, 1943 aged 33.
He was the son of Henry W. and Agnes M. Parkes; husband of Violet Emily Ada Parkes, of Hayes.
The 72nd. Regiment was attached to the Headquarters of the British 1st. Army. They had landed in North Africa in November 1942, and had driven the Axis forces out of Africa by May, 43 and were now waiting to be transferred to 8th. Army to take part in the invasion of Sicily targeted for July.
He died as a "result of accidental drowning whilst taking part in organised bathing".
He is buried at Medjez-el-Bab War Cemetery, Tunisia, Grave 7. H. 1.

PARKER Thomas
Private 3321776 1st. Battalion, Gordon Highlanders, who died on Tuesday, 15th. August, 1944 aged 27.
He was the son of Arthur B. and Anne N. Parker; husband of Dorothy Parker, of Hayes.
The 1st. Battalion was part of 153rd. Brigade of the 51st. Highland Infantry Division, one of the most experienced in the British Army. The Germans had launched their counter-attack on the American breakout at St. Lo. but had left their flank exposed to the British and Canadian forces. The Allies now proceeded to attack southwards and hoped to link up with the Americans, and cut off the Germans in what was to be known as the Falaise Gap. Thomas died in the fighting on the 15th. and the Canadians captured Falaise on the 16th. But the Germans had already commenced their retreat and escaped over the Seine which the Allies in hot pursuit, crossed on the 24th.of August, racing on to Brussels. The Belgians did not realise they had been liberated until they woke up in the morning and saw British tanks instead of what they thought were German.
He is buried at Ranville War Cemetery, Calvados, France. Grave IX. F. 8.

PARSONS George E. H.
Leading Cook C/MX 54986 H.M.S. *Tempest* Royal Navy, who died on Monday, 23rd. February, 1942.
The *Tempest* was a 'T' class submarine of 1000/1575 tons displacement and was launched in June 1941. She had a complement of 63, 11 torpedo tubes, carried 17 torpedoes, and had a speed of 12 knots on the surface and 9 submerged.
Tempest was sunk as a result of an attack on the Italian tanker *Lucania* on the 12th. February by the submarine HMS *Una*. *Lucania* had been given a "safe conduct" pass by the British because she was engaged on humanitarian work, and thus the Italians were exceedingly angry that she had been sunk. Extra patrols were instituted in the Gulf of Taranto to find the culprit but *Tempest* was the unlucky recipient of their attentions. At 0315 hrs. on the 13th. the torpedo boat *Circe* got an Asdic contact with *Tempest* and then carried out seven hours of depth-charge attacks which reduced the inside of the submarine to a shambles.
At 0942 hrs. with No.3 battery producing great clouds of toxic chlorine gas the captain Lt. Cdr. *Cavaye* gave the order to surface. Machine gun fire from the *Circe* prevented *Tempest's* crew bringing either the 4 in. gun or their machine guns into action, so *Cavaye* gave the order to open the main vents and set the scuttling charges, before giving the order to abandon ship. The survivors were picked up by the *Circe* but *Tempest* remained stubbornly afloat until 1605 hrs. when she sunk, just as *Circe's* crew managed to secure a tow rope.
George was one of the survivors who were picked up, but he died of his wounds in one of the local hospitals ten days later . The *Tempest* had 39 fatalities and 24 survivors.
He is buried at Bari War Cemetery, Italy. Grave VII. E. 38, and commemorated at St. Mary's, Hayes

PEACOCK John Winter   DCM   MM
Lieutenant 11th. Hussars, Royal Armoured Corps, who died on Friday, 23rd. October, 1942 aged 22.
He was the son of Joseph S. and Nellie E. Peacock, of Hayes End.
"The 11th. Hussars, the famous *Cherry Pickers*, were undoubtedly the finest armoured car recognisance regiment in the British Army." They were part of the 7th. Armoured Division (The Desert Rats), and were carrying out reconnaissance before the diversionary attack in the south of the Alamein position started on the 25th. John was killed on one of these patrols
He is buried at El Alamein War Cemetery, Egypt. Grave XXVII. E. 3.
He was a very brave young man and is the only soldier in Hillingdon to receive two awards for gallantry.

Entry in the London Gazette, 8th. July, 1941
"Sergeant John Winter Peacock was awarded the Military Medal for distinguished service in the Middle East from December 1940 to February, 1941".
Amazingly on the same page
"Corporal Alfred George **WADHAM** of the King's Royal Rifle Corps and of Hayes, Middx. was awarded the Military Medal". There is no record of him in the Commonwealth War Graves Register so it can be assumed that he survived the war.
Entry in the London Gazette of 24th. February 1942, states,
"Sergeant John Winter Peacock, M.M. was awarded the Distinguished Conduct Medal for gallant and distinguished service in the Middle East".

To avoid repetition I detail below a note compiled from the various histories of -

The Battle of El Alamein

In June 1942 *Rommel* and *Panzerarmee Afrika* had taken Tobruk and the Eighth Army were in full retreat, and Rommel was driving his men on towards Cairo and Alexandria. Lt. General *Montgomery* replaced *Auchinleck* and the re-equipped and revitalised Eighth Army had halted *Rommel's* last desperate attempt to reach the Nile Delta in the battle of Alam Halfa, fought at the end of August.

With Egypt now secure, and *Panzerarmee Afrika* in a desperate supply situation (its main supply base and port of Tripoli was over a 1,000 miles away to the west, *Montgomery* could plan his own offensive to, as he puts it, "hit *Rommel* for six right out of Africa." The Alamein position was unique in the Western desert because it had secure flanks, resting on the sea in the north and the Qattara Depression in the south. This the 37 miles of front could easily be held by both armies. *Montgomery's* plan was to mount a direct assault in the north, near the coast. The Axis forces dug themselves in and used vast amounts of mines and booby traps up to five miles deep to make the attack fail. After a massive artillery bombardment, the infantry and sappers would make the breaches in the defences, and as the British had far more tanks than the Axis, for them to break through regardless of the losses they sustained in men and material, what *Montgomery* would call a "dogfight". This *Montgomery* estimated would last 12 days,

The opening attack "Operation Lightfoot" began on the late evening of the 23rd. October, 1942 with the bombardment. The infantry attack had bitten deeply into the Axis lines, but by dawn on the 24th.there were still fewer gaps in their lines than was expected. The two armoured divisions, the 1st. and 10th. were ordered by *Montgomery* to push on and suffer the heavy losses.

On the 25th feint attacks in the south by the 7th. Armoured and 50th. Infantry divisions took place but they suffered heavy casualties and the attack was called off on the 27th. to avoid further losses. *Montgomery* pulled out the 10th. Armoured division and ordered an attack northwards by the 1st. Armoured and 9th Australian Infantry divisions, whilst continuing the attacks along the line to *crumble* the enemy's defence. *Rommel* now launched his armour with fierce counter-attacks, but they were repelled.

On the 30 and 31st. the Australians launched another attack towards the coast, but suffered heavy casualties but were able to hang on in face of these fierce attacks, but they were not successful.

On the 2nd. November, *Montgomery* started the final offensive, Operation *Supercharge* and after heavy fighting 1st. Armoured broke through. The Axis were able to halt the Allies but *Rommel* realised he was beaten and began the withdrawal, and on the 4th. November the Allied tanks had broken out in the open desert, and the battle was over.

Eighth Army had suffered 13,500 casualties and lost 500 tanks, but *Panzerarmee Afrika* had been smashed and over 35,000 prisoners taken. By January 23rd. Tripoli had fallen and the race to link up with the American and British Armies in Tunis began.
As Churchill said "it might almost be said that before Alamein we never had a victory, while after Alamein we never had a defeat".

PEARSON Vincent
Rifleman 5255843 7th. (1st. Battalion The London Irish Rifles) Battalion, Rifle Brigade, who died on Wednesday, 31st. March, 1943 aged 27.
He was the husband of Alice Dorothy Pearson, of Hayes.
The 1st. Battalion was part of the 7th. Motor Brigade of the 1st. Armoured Division, who had as part of 8th. Army advanced from Egypt to Tunisia. Now they were confronted by the old Mareth Line which the French had built to prevent the Italians invading from Libya. The Axis had taken it over and strengthened the defences.
Montgomery's original plan was to make a frontal attack with XXX Corps and a diversionary attack on the Axis right flank with the New Zealand Division. The frontal attack began on the 20th. March but was not successful, being driven back by the Panzers. *Montgomery* now changed his plans and switched 1st. Armoured to support the New Zealanders. It was a complete success, and under heavy Allied air attacks the Germans withdrew on March 26th. Vincent was wounded in this battle and died later.
Eighth Army went on to capture Sfax, link up with the Allied 1st. Army make the final drive to capture Tunis and force the Axis to surrender on May 7th.
He is buried at Sfax War Cemetery, Tunisia. Grave X1V. C. 9. Sfax is 270 kms, south of Tunis.

PEGGS Ernest John
Corporal 6106289 2/5th. Battalion, The Queen's Royal Regiment (West Surrey), who died on Saturday, 2nd. September, 1944 aged 22.
He was the son of Thomas A. and Rose N. Peggs, of Hayes.
The Queens was part of the 35th. Infantry Brigade of the 56th. Infantry Division who had landed at Salerno in September 1943, captured Naples and taken part in the Battle for Cassino and advanced northwards, He died in the advance from Ancona to Rimini which broke the *Gothic Line*, the main German defensive position in the north of Italy and the heavy fighting around Rimini which fell on the 21st. September.
He is buried at Gradara War Cemetery, Italy. Grave 11. B.31. This cemetery is situated midway between Pesaro and Riccione and contains the graves of 1200 casualties from these battles. He is commemorated at St. Mary's, Hayes.

PENN William Wallace
Serjeant 6287173 2nd. Battalion The Buffs (Royal East Kent Regiment), who died on Friday, 26th. January, 1945 aged 26.
He was the son of William and Mabel Penn; nephew of Mrs. A. J. Walker, of Ealing.
The Buffs were part of the 6th. Independent Indian Infantry Division which had served in the Middle East in 1943/44 and arrived in India on the 1st. August, 1944. They moved to Assam and the Burma borders in January, 1945 The Allies crossed the river Irrawaddy on the 14th. January and William's division moved into Burma on the 31st. January, but unfortunately William died in the early fighting. He is buried at Taukkyan War Cemetery, Burma (now Myanmar) Grave 27. G.5. and commemorated at St. Mary's, Hayes. Taukkyan is outside Rangoon and is the largest cemetery in Burma and was begun in 1951 by bringing in the graves from the scattered burial grounds so that they could be properly maintained.

PERRYMAN George Sidney

Lance Bombardier 1090060 64 (The Queen's Own Royal Glasgow Yeomanry) Anti-Tank Regiment, Royal Artillery, who died on Monday 15th. May, 1944 aged 29.

He was the son of George W. and Caroline Perryman; husband of Joan Perryman, of Hayes Bridge, Hayes.

The 64th. were the divisional artillery of the 78th. Infantry (Battleaxe) Division. Monte Cassino was the lynch pin of the *Gustav Line* which the Axis had built across Italy. Since January the Allies had been trying to breach this line, link up with the Anzio beachhead and capture Rome. Operation *Diadem* stared on the 11th. May, with the crossing of the Rapido river after a huge bombardment, with the 78th. as the follow up troops. On the second night two bridges had been built across the river and the 78th were across and advancing rapidly. George died in this advance but on the 16th. the Germans abandoned the Gustav Line, and withdrew to the north of Rome, which fell on the 5th. June.

He is buried at Cassino War Cemetery, Italy. Grave X1. K. 2.

PETTET Cecil Edward

Leading Wireman D/MX 73584 H.M.S. *Copra*, Royal Navy, who died on Wednesday, 7th. June, 1944 aged 24.

He was the son of Harry and Phyllis A. Pettet, of Hayes End.

H.M.S. *Cobra* was the 592 Landing Craft Assault Flotilla and they were taking part in the Normandy landings which had started on the 6th. June. He died on the second day and was then brought home for burial at Hayes and Harlington (Cherry Lane) Cemetery. Sec W. 1. Grave A 2. Cecil is commemorated at St. Mary's, Hayes.

PHAIR Sidney Alfred

Private 5950016 5th. Battalion, Bedfordshire and Hertfordshire Regiment, who died on Monday, 22nd. November, 1943 aged 25.

He was the son of William S. and Louisa A. Phair. His wife lived in Rowan Place, West Avenue, Hayes. and in civilian life he was a landscape gardener.

The 5th Battalion was part of the 55th.Brigade of the 18th. Infantry Division (see note after Gerald **GREEN**) and he was taken prisoner when Singapore fell on the 15th. February, 1942. He was sent to work on the Burma-Siam railway and died in captivity

He is buried at Kanchanaburi War Cemetery, Thailand. Grave 2. B. 53, and commemorated at St. Mary's. Hayes.

See after **BALL W. F.** for note on Burma-Siam Railway.

PHIPPS Alan Reginald

Sergeant 1895140 R.A.F.V.R. who died on Saturday, 24th. March, 1945 aged 20.

He was the son of Reginald T. and Lillian M. Phipps, of Hayes.

He was a Flight Engineer flying Stirling V s with 46 Squadron based at Stones Cross, Hants, near Southampton. The Stirlings had been converted from heavy bombers and were now being used as troop transports. They had carried out a trip to Castel Benito, Libya. (just south of Tripoli) on the 23rd. But on the return trip they crashed in Southern France and all the crew of nine were killed. They are buried at Mazargues War Cemetery, Marseilles, France. Plot 3. Row E. Collective grave 8-16.

POLLARD John Gorringe

Flight Sergeant 1319182 R.A.F.V.R. who died on Monday, 21st. February, 1944.
He was a navigator flying Mosquito XV111 with 618 Squadron at Predannack, Lizard, Cornwall.
He was transferred to 143 Squadron at North Coates, Lincs. and was carrying out tests when his aircraft crashed into the sea. Both he and the pilot Flying Officer Caron (a Frenchman) ditched successfully but their dinghy was never seen again and they were both lost.
He is commemorated on the Runnymede Memorial, Panel 221 and St. Mary's, Hayes..

POLLARD Leonard James

Gunner 988686 Royal Artillery, who died on Tuesday, 12th. December, 1944 aged 24.
He was the son of Thomas S. and Ellen R. Pollard. of Weymouth Road Hayes.
He died of pulmonary tuberculosis at Weymouth Road. In civilian life he was an optical frame maker.
He is buried at Islington Cemetery, Middx. Sec. L. Block 9. Grave 17408P. and commemorated at St. Mary's, Hayes.

PORTSMOUTH Ronald Arthur

Gunner 1801666 242 Battery, 48 Light Anti-Aircraft Regiment, Royal Artillery, who died on Monday, 9th. July, 1945 aged 25,
He was the son of Arthur and Phoebe Portsmouth, of Devonshire Place, Harlington.
The 38 Light A. A. Regiment left the United Kingdom on the 6th. December 1941 for overseas and with the invasion of Malaya by the Japanese was diverted to Java. They arrived there on the 3rd. February, but the Japanese overrun the island and he was captured on the 12th. March 1942.
He was being transferred to Japan when the ship he was on board was sunk by U. S. carrier planes or submarines. This was a month before the dropping of the two atom bombs on Hiroshima and Nagasaki. He was a builder's assistant in civilian life.
He is commemorated on the Singapore Memorial. Column 28, St. Mary's. Harmondsworth, and St. Peter's and St. Paul's, Harlington.

PRINCE John Coleman

Pilot Officer 201082 R.A.F.V.R. who died on Tuesday, 30th. October, 1945 aged 23.
He was the son of Thomas and Hilda A. Prince, of Hayes.
He was with 1653 Heavy Conversion Unit based at Chedburgh, Suffolk. He was a second pilot flying Lancasters and was killed in a flying accident.
He is commemorated on the Runnymede Memorial Panel 268, St. Mary's. Hayes, and St. Peter's and St. Paul's Harlington.

PRIOR Albert Horace

Lance Bombardier 11003401 90 Light Anti-Aircraft Regiment, Royal Artillery, who died on Thursday, 17th. February, 1944 aged 38.
He was the son of George W. and Lillian S. Prior; husband of Edith Louisa Prior, of Hayes.
The 90th were part of the divisional artillery of the 1st. Infantry Division (not to be confused with 1st. London Division) and Albert was killed in one of the German counter-attacks.
Please see note after Thomas **CLARE**.
He is buried at Anzio War Cemetery, Italy. Grave 11. P. 12.

PRYCE William
Sapper 6853752 238 Field Company, Royal Engineers, who died on Friday, 8th. December, 1944 aged 22.
He was the son of William and Frances Ethel Pryce, of Hayes.
The 238 Field Company was part of the 1st. London Infantry Division who arrived in Italy on the 17th. July, 1944. They were now engaged in the heavy fighting near Forli, which took place between the 8th, and 12th, south of Ravenna, trying to cross the river Lamone . William died in this battle and although initially successful, such was the stubbornness of the German resistance that Bologna did not fall until the 21st. April, 1945.
He is buried at Bologna War Cemetery, Italy. Grave 1. B. 1, and commemorated at St. Mary's, Hayes.

RAWLINGS Cyril Walter Henry
Sergeant 1391939 R.A.F.V.R. who died on Sunday 28th. March, 1943 aged 30.
He was the husband of Rose May Rawlings, of Hayes.
He was an Observer with 42 Operational Training Unit flying Blenheim 1 s from Andover. The Blenheim crashed at Lavington Folly, Wilts at 1115hrs.on the 28th. March. He was admitted to Tidworth Hospital where he died.
He is buried at Hayes and Harlington (Cherry Lane) Cemetery, Sec C. 1. Grave N.28, and commemorated at St. Peter's and St. Paul's, Harlington.

READ George Edward Henry Charles
Driver T/76128 2 Corps Petrol Park, Royal Army Service Corps, who died on Tuesday, 19th. March, 1940 aged 26.
He was the son of Mrs. E. Read and stepson of Mr. F. Packer, of Hayes End.
He died from a fractured skull at No. 8 Casualty Clearing Station following a traffic accident.
He is buried at Fouquieres Churchyard Extension, Pas de Calais. Plot 4. Row K. Grave 12.

REDFERN Eric Arthur
Flight Sergeant R.A.F.V.R. 754894 who died on Sunday, 17th. August, 1941 aged 27.
He was a pilot flying Hurricane 1 s with 242 Squadron of 11 Group from Manston, Kent. He took off in the evening with his Squadron to take part in a *Roadsteading* operation, which was low level attack on coastal shipping in the Channel. .He was shot down by an Me. 109 as was P.O. K.M. Hick of the same squadron.
He is buried at Etaples Military Cemetery. Grave 46. D 1. Etaples is a town 27 kms. south of Boulogne and because it was the site of the hospitals during WW1 has the graves of 11,430 Commonwealth casualties. Eric is commemorated at St. Mary's, Hayes.

RHODES John Charles
Flight Sergeant 1323234 R.A.F.V.R. who died on Monday, 15th. May, 1944 aged 23.
He was the son of Benjamin and Lillian A. Rhodes; husband of Georgina Margaret Rhodes, of Hayes.
He was a Navigator / Wireless Operator flying Beaufighter X s with 603 Squadron based at Gambut, Libya, which is near Bardia. He took off with his pilot F/Sgt. Paddison and 3 other Beaufighters on Operation *Bricklayer*, the object of which was to destroy the German radar system in the Aegean Sea. They swept the central Aegean, strafing Tenos harbour and they then attacked the airstrip at Papos, but were hit by the intense flak and broke in two, bursting into flames when they hit the ground.
He and the pilot are buried at Phaleron War Cemetery, Athens, Greece. Collective grave 23. D. 15.

RICHARDS Norman Louis
Sergeant 1604532 R.A.F.V.R. who died on Tuesday, 27th. June, 1944 aged 20.
He was the son of Louis T. and Elsie M. Richards, of Hayes.
He was an Air Bomber with No. 10 (Observers) Advanced Flying Unit based at Montrose, Scotland.
He lost his life when his Anson twin engined trainer collided with another Anson at Solway Firth, 2 miles south west of Southerness point at 0835 hrs.
He is buried at Hayes and Harlington (Cherry Lane) Cemetery. Sec C.3. Grave A.14, and is commemorated at St. Mary's, Hayes, and St. Peter's and St. Paul's, Harlington.

RIDOUT Robert
Gunner 897313 117 Field Regiment, Royal Artillery who died on Tuesday, 14th. April, 1942 aged 20.
He was the son of Robert and Mary A. Ridout, of Cromwell Road, Hayes End.
He died from an infection after an operation at the Royal Victoria Hospital. Netley, Hants.   In civilian life he was formerly a messenger.
He is buried at Netley Military Cemetery, Hants, Grave 2209.

RIELLY Gordon Keith
Private 14499103 1/5th. Battalion, The Queen's Royal Regiment (West Surrey), who died on Thursday, 20th. July, 1944 aged 18.
He was the son of William H. and Elizabeth Rielly, of Hayes.
The West Surreys was part of the 131st. Infantry Brigade of the 7th. Armoured Division, the Desert Rats who had landed in Normandy on the 10th. June.   He died in the heavy fighting of Operation *Goodwood* (Please see note after Joseph **NORMAN** for the full details).
He is buried at La Delivrande War Cemetery, Douvres, Calvados. Grave 111. J. 1, and commemorated at St. Mary's, Hayes.

RIXON Percy Alfonso
Private 6298859 5th. Battalion, The Buffs (Royal East Kent Regiment), who died on Thursday, 8th. April, 1943 aged 27.
He was the husband of Margaret Alice Rixon.
The battalion was part of the 36th. Infantry Brigade of the 78th. (Battleaxe) Infantry Division who had landed on the 11th. November, 1942, 3 days after D-Day in North Africa.   They had advanced across Algeria and Tunisia and were now about to take part in the final battles.   They were a "Mountain" division and were tasked to seize the heights above Medjez el Bab which was the gateway to the city of Tunis.   This they succeeded in doing but Percy died in the close fighting.
Also taking part in this battle was a certain comedian called *Spike Milligan* who was in the 56th. Heavy Regiment, Royal Artillery, who were supporting the attack.
On the 12th. May. *Von Arnim* surrendered and it was the end of the Axis in North Africa, with 150, 000 Axis troops going into captivity.
He is buried at Qued Zarga War Cemetery, Tunisia. Grave 1.J.10, and commemorated at St. Mary's, Hayes.

ROBBINS Edward Elmer
Pilot Officer 143470 R.A.F.V.R. who died on Sunday, 8th. November, 1942 aged 22.
He was the son of Elmer and Edith Robbins; husband of Irene Mary Robbins, of Hayes.
He was a navigator flying Hudson 111 twin engined general purpose aircraft with 233 Squadron based at Gibraltar.   On the 8th. November the Allies began their invasion of Morocco and Algeria

(Operation *Torch*). They were with four other Hudsons from the Squadron giving anti-submarine protection to the American forces under General *Patten* who were landing at Casablanca. Four of the aircraft failed to return and although the squadron records are silent, it must be assumed that they were shot down by Vichy French fighters, as the Germans and Italians had no aircraft in the area at that time.

He is commemorated on the Malta Memorial. Panel 3, Column 1.

ROBERTS Clifford William

Trooper 6850599 The Queen's Bays (2nd. Dragoon Guards), Royal Armoured Corps, who died on Saturday, 24th. October, 1942 aged 21.

He was the son of Bertie and Annie J. Roberts, of Hayes.

Please see note on Alamein battle after John **PEACOCK**

The Queen's Bays was part of the 1st. Armoured Division and consisted of 92 Sherman and 1 Grant tanks. These were the latest American tanks and were more than a match for Panzer Mark 3 and 4 s, with which the Germans were equipped.

Clifford died on the second day of the battle when Eighth Army were trying to clear passages in the Axis lines, to enable the tanks to break out,

He is commemorated on the Alamein Memorial. Column 16.

ROBERTS Ronald Frank

Flight Sergeant 1301559 R.A.F.V.R. who died on Tuesday 24th. August, 1943 aged 22,

He was the son of Reginald and Clarressa V. Roberts, of Hayes End.

He was an Air Bomber flying Halifax 11 s with 102 Squadron of 4 Group based at Pocklington, Yorks. They took off at 2026 hrs. to bomb Berlin. They crashed in the North Sea, and the pilot Sgt. G.S. Roadley's body was recovered from the sea, but the other six of the crew including Ronald are commemorated on the Runnymede Memorial, Panel 138.

727 aircraft were despatched and it was the most serious raid of the war on Berlin to date. 56 aircraft failed to return. The Battle of Berlin was to start in mid-November and continued to the end of March 1944 with the R.A.F. sustaining heavy losses and not achieving the results they wanted because Berlin was outside the range of *Oboe*.(A radio beam blind bombing system made by EMI at Feltham.)

RODDEN John Alexander

Corporal 3596875 2nd. Battalion, The London Irish Rifles, Royal Ulster Rifles, who died on Thursday, 5th, August, 1943 aged 33.

He was the son of Hugh and Edith A. Rodden; husband of Jenny Rodden, of Hayes.

The 2nd Battalion was part of 38th. Irish Infantry Brigade of the 78th. (Battleaxe) Infantry Division. They had landed in Algeria in November 1942 and had help drive the Axis out of Africa. On the 10th. July Sicily was invaded by the Combined American and British forces. The Battleaxe Division was held in reserve and when Montgomery realised his advance on the east side of Sicily was being held up by the Herman Goering Division he sent for them, and they arrived on the 25th. July; the same day that Mussolini was deposed.

They helped take the town of Centuripe and advanced on the west side of Mount Etna. John died in the initial attacks on Randazzo. Mount Macerone was then taken and they linked up with the US 9th Division advancing from the north. This was the end of the Division's fighting in Sicily, which was by the end of August in Allied hands.

He is buried at Catania War Cemetery, Sicily, Grave 1V. F. 1.and commemorated at St. Mary's Hayes.

ROGERS Eric Frederick
Sergeant 1850097 R.A.F.V.R. who died on Thursday, 2nd. August, 1945 aged 21.
He was the son of William F. and Edith R. Rogers, of Hayes.
He was a navigator serving with 216 Group, which was a Communication Squadron based at Heliopolis, Egypt. He died in a flying accident when his Liberator four engined American Bomber/Transport crashed at 2140 hrs. 200 yards west of R.A.F. Lydda, Palestine.
He is buried at Ramleh War Cemetery, Israel. Grave 7.B. 6, and commemorated at St. Mary's, Hayes and St. Peter's and St. Paul's, Harlington. Ramleh, now Ramla is 12kms. south east of Jaffa.

ROLFE Leslie George
Trooper 306505 Royal Horse Guards, The Household Cavalry who died on Saturday, 3rd. November 1945 aged 18.
He was the son of Frederick G. and Violet M. Rolfe, of Hayes.
He died from an accidental gun shot to his neck.
He is buried at Southern Cemetery, Cologne, Germany. Plot 7. Row F. Grave 25, and commemorated at St. Mary's, Hayes.

ROLFE Ronald John
Sergeant 1850207 R.A.F.V.R. who died on Thursday,15th. June, 1944 aged 21.
He was the grandson of Mrs. C.L. Huse, of Slough, Bucks.
He was a Flight Engineer flying Lancaster 1 s with 15 Squadron of 3 Group based at Mildenhall, Suffolk. They took off at 2331 hrs. as part of the second wave to bomb Le Havre and were shot down over France, the only aircraft lost on the raid. The Air Bomber survived, four of the crew were lost at sea and are commemorated at Runnymede and he and the Wireless Operator are buried at Fecamp (Le Val Aux Clercs) Communal Cemetery, British Plot. Row 1. His grave is 2.
Fecamp is a seaport 41 kms. north-east of Le Havre. He is commemorated at St. Mary's, Hayes.
As the first wave took off in the evening and with the short distance to the target, Bomber Command regarded it as a daylight raid, their first since May 1943 when the light Bombers left for Fighter Command. 221 Lancasters and 13 Mosquitoes were sent and their objective was the fast German motor-torpedo boats (E-Boats) who were threatening the Normandy beaches 30 miles away. The port area was hit with 1230 tons of bombs and few E-boats remained undamaged. The Dam Buster Squadron's 22 Lancasters had even dropped their 12,000 lb. *Tallboy* bomb causing great damage.

ROWLEY George William
Leading Aircraftman 1464399 R.A.F.V.R. who died on Wednesday, 29th. November, 1944.
He was the son of Mr. and Mrs. William Rowley; husband of Betty Ivy Rowley, of Hayes.
He was a Radio Operator at Headquarters 239 Wing in Italy. He was killed when a bomb, believed to have fallen from a friendly aircraft, exploded in the town of Fano at 1410 hrs. He was admitted to 58 General Hospital but died at 1700 hrs.
He is buried at Ancona War Cemetery, Italy. Grave 111. H 1, and commemorated at St. Mary's. Hayes.

RUSSELL Edward Charles Thomas
Signalman 2382908 Royal Corps of Signals, who died on Tuesday, 11th. July, 1944 aged 22.
He was the son of Charles and Gladys I. Russell, of Hayes.
He was attached to the 4th. Armoured Brigade, who arrived in Normandy on D+1, the 7th. June.
They were attached to the British 8 Corps.
For details of his death please see note on Normandy after **Kenneth BEEBE**.

71

He is buried at St. Manvieu War Cemetery, Cheux, Calvados. Grave 1X. C. 19, and commemorated at St. Mary's. Hayes.

RUSSELL Frank Arthur
Private 14563033 12th.(Airborne) Battalion, Devonshire Regiment who died on Saturday, 26th. August, 1944 aged 28.
The Devons were part of the 6th. Airlanding Brigade of the 6th.Airborne Division. They were landed by glider on D-Day on the left flank of the Allied landings and were tasked to hold defensive positions on the east bank of the Caen Canal and the river Orne.
This they successfully did for 10 weeks, and with Falaise falling, on the 19th. were chasing the Germans back into Belgium and Holland. Frank died in the final battles, and the Allies crossed the Seine on the 26th.
The Airborne forces were withdrawn to the U.K. on the 3rd. September, and did not return to the continent until Christmas. Their object was to halt the German advance in the Ardennes and prepare for the crossing of the Rhine and the advance into Germany
Frank is buried at St. Desir War Cemetery, Calvados, Grave V. A. 1. St, Desir is 4 kms. west of Lisieux, and east of Caen. There are 594 casualties buried here, most of whom died chasing the Germans towards the Seine. He is also commemorated at St. Mary's, Hayes.

SALTER Kenneth William
Private 11684609 Royal Army Ordnance Corps who died on Sunday, 9th. May, 1943 aged 26.
He was the son of Charles J. and Louie Salter, of Hayes.
The final battle for Tunisia was taking place and Von Arnim surrendered on the 12th. May, and 100,000 Axis soldiers were taken prisoner. During this period many of the soldiers were relaxing after a long and difficult campaign. They would go swimming in the sea, and unfortunately Kenneth was drowned.
He is buried at Bone War Cemetery, Annaba, Algeria. Grave 1. E. 12. Annaba is a seaport in North-East Algeria and was quite a long way to the rear of the fighting in Tunisia. He is commemorated at St. Mary's Hayes.

SAMUELS Reginald Douglas
Sergeant 1321353 R.A.F.V.R. who died on Wednesday, 15th. March, 1944 aged 22.
He was the son of Harold and Sarah Samuels, of Hayes.
He was a navigator flying Lancaster 1 s with 550 Squadron of 1 Group based at North Killingholme, Lincs. They took off at 1911 hrs. to bomb Stuttgart, but crashed on the outward leg near Appenwihr (Haut-Rhin), roughly 8 kms. from the centre of Colmar, France. The crew of seven all died and are buried at Cholloy War Cemetery, Meurthe-et-Moselle, France. 4 A. Collective grave 12-18. Cholloy is 28kms. west of Nancy.
863 aircraft were despatched and the outward leg took them over France and they then turned north east at the Swiss border to approach Stuttgart from the south. 27 aircraft were lost but the bombing was reasonably successful.

SAVILLE John
Driver T/14648665 Royal Army Service Corps, who died on Monday, 11th. September, 1944 aged 34.
He was the son of Henry W. and Emma Saville; husband of Edith Lilian Saville, of Hayes.
As no unit is detailed it is difficult to trace exactly where John died. Falaise had fallen on the 15th. August, and the Allies had crossed the Seine on the 25th. They were in Brussels on the 3rd. September and were preparing for Operation Market-Garden, the Airborne drop on Arnhem etc.,

which took place on the 17th. St Desir War Cemetery is the most eastern of the Normandy cemeteries and as the German Airforce had virtually ceased to exist, John was probably killed in the advance from Normandy by German rearguards.

He is buried at St. Desir War Cemetery, Calvados, France. Grave 11. A. 4, and commemorated at St. Mary's. Hayes.

SCOTT John Alfred
Private S/210886 Royal Army Service Corps, who died on Monday 4th. June, 1945 aged 27.
He was the son of Thomas and Emma Scott, of Hayes.
"He died of drowning in Italy" Probably swimming from the beaches of Salerno.
He is buried at Salerno War Cemetery. Italy. Grave V11. A. 19.

SEARLE Charles Benjamin
Firewatcher, who died on Wednesday, 19th. February, 1941 aged 39.
He died at his own home, 9 Botwell Crescent, Hayes. His wife G.M. Searle survived him.
This is the same night that the bomb fell in Longmead Road killing ten people and could have been in the same "stick" of bombs, dropped by one aircraft. See entry under Charles **DEAMER.**
He is commemorated at St. Mary's, Hayes.

SHAW John Cecil   Mentioned in Despatches.
Sergeant 742749 R.A.F.V.R,. who died on Sunday, 4th. January, 1942 aged 23.
He was the son of John and Elizabeth C. Shaw, of Hayes.
He was a pilot flying twin engined Hampden bombers with 49 Squadron of 5 Group based at Scampton, Lincs. They took off to attack airfields in Northern France but were hit by flak and crash-landed in northern France. All four members of the crew were taken prisoner.
He was shot and killed whilst trying to escape, at Barth, Germany. Barth is a town on the Baltic coast north west of Rostock. Interestingly enough, it has an aerodrome.
He is buried at Berlin 1939-1945 War Cemetery, Berlin. Grave 8. L. 30 This was a reburial after the war ended, when all the graves were centralised.
The London Gazette 2nd. June, 1943
The King has been graciously pleased to give orders for the publication of the name of the following person who have been mentioned in despatches by the Air Officer Commanding.
Sergeant J.C. Shaw

SHERVILL Herbert James
Private 6411104 2nd Battalion, Royal Sussex Regiment, who died on Friday, 13th. August, 1943 aged 28.
He was the son of Thomas and Susan Shervill; husband of Alma Victoria Beattie Shervill, of Hillingdon Heath, Uxbridge.
The 2nd. Battalion was part of *PALFORCE* (Palestine) and was formed in September, 1942 under the command of 10th. Army and consisted mainly of three infantry battalions. Their task was to protect the oilfields of Iraq and Iran, and the railway carrying supplies to Russia from the Persian Gulf.
He was killed as the "result of an explosion" and is buried at Tehran War Cemetery, Iran. Grave 6.C.10, and commemorated at St. Mary's, Hayes.
Please see note after **M.F.A. Hickman**

SHEWRY Cyril Joseph
Sergeant 550468 R.A.F. who died on Wednesday, 22nd. May, 1940 aged 21.
He was the son of Cyril G. and Doris M. Shewry, of Hayes End.
He was a Observer flying Hampden 1 s (twin engined bombers) with 144 Squadron of 5 Group based at Hemswell, Norfolk. They took from Hemswell to bomb Krefield. Hit by flak over the target area, the crew were ordered to bale out. Three did so, though Cyril was killed, but the other two were captured and became POW s. The pilot, P/O Coton, then regained control and flew the Hampden back to England. However, as he crossed the East Anglia coast his aircraft was caught in searchlights and he baled out, leaving the aircraft to crash near Raynham, Essex. 124 aircraft were despatched that night and 5 failed to return to base.
He is buried at the Reichswald Forest War Cemetery, Kleve, Nordrhein-Westfalen, Germany. Grave 28. E. 5.

SIMMONS Stephen Thomas
Chief Motor Mechanic 4th. Class P/MX 99023 *H.M.M.T.B. 278* Royal Navy who died on Monday, 28th. June, 1943 aged 29.
He was the son of Henry G. and Rosanna Simmons; husband of Mary Eleanor Maud Simmons, of Hayes.
His Majesties Motor Torpedo Boat 278 was not sunk and the only information on his Death Certificate is that he died "on war service". It is probably safe to assume he died of natural causes, as the Japanese fleet was heavily involved fighting the Americans in the Solomon Islands, thousands of miles away.
He is buried at Calcutta (Bhowanipore) Cemetery. India. Plot L. Grave 60, and commemorated at St. Mary's, Hayes.

SIMPSON Charles James
Corporal 5504406 1/4th. Battalion, Hampshire Regiment, who died on Sunday, 20th. February, 1944 aged 24.
He was the son of James J. and Florence M. Simpson, of Hayes.
The Hampshires were part of the 128th. Infantry Brigade of the 46th. Infantry Division who landed at Salerno on the 9th. September, 1943 and took part in the fighting at Naples, the crossing of the river Volturno, and the early battles against the *Gustav* Lime, which ran completely across Italy. They were now taking part in the advance on the West coast, up Route 7 from Capua to Rome, and crossing the Carigliano near Minturno, which was the eastern end of the *Gustav* Line. The attack began on the 11th. January and the Carigliano was crossed on the 17th. and the building of bridges began. But the Germans counter-attacked, the Allies withdrew and Charles died in this heavy fighting.
The advance did not recommence until May, 1944.
He is buried at Minturno War Cemetery, Italy. Grave 11. A. 22. Minturno is 78 kms. north of Naples.

SIMPSON Stanley
Private 14684235 7th. Battalion, Seaforth Highlanders, who died on Tuesday, 11th. July, 1944 aged 19.
He was the son of James S. and Florence Simpson, of Hayes.
The Seaforths were part of the 46th. Brigade of 15th. (Scottish) Infantry Division who had arrived in Normandy on the 17th. June, 1944.
For details of his death please see note after **Kenneth BEEBE**.

He is buried at Ryles War Cemetery, Bazenville, Calvados. Grave V1. E.7. and commemorated at St. Mary's, Hayes.

SIMPSON William Murray
Craftsman 7654443 attached Royal Artillery, who died on Friday 8th. September, 1944 aged 37.
He was the son of Mr. and Mrs. Alexander Simpson; husband of Maisie Simpson, of Hayes.
After the Falaise Gap battles the Germans were in full retreat, and the Allies advanced north from Normandy into Belgium. On the 3rd. September they entered Brussels. and on the 4th. Antwerp fell. But *Goering* had been able to create a Parachute Army from the Luftwaffe ground staff and rushed them to defend Belgium. They were placed under the command of General *Student* and thus there now took place the "Battle of the Canals", as the Germans desperately tried to halt the Allies advance. William died in this heavy fighting.
He is buried at Geel War Cemetery, Antwerp, Belgium. Grave 11. C. 6. and commemorated at St. Mary's, Hayes.

SLAUGHTER Edward Crone
Flight Sergeant 1682293 R.A.F.V.R. who died on Thursday, 8th. February, 1945 aged 24.
He was the son of Edward J. and Elizabeth J. of South Shields, Co. Durham, and husband of Alice Devonport Slaughter, of Hayes.
He was an Air Bomber flying Lancaster 111s with 57 Squadron, of 5 Group based at East Kirkby, Lincs. He was flying in the same aircraft as **Donald APLIN** also of Hayes (please see above).
He is buried at Helsingborg (Palsjo) Municipal Cemetery, Sweden, Section XV, Grave 84B.

SMITH Ernest George
Lance Corporal 1734278 Corps of Military Police, who died on Friday 28th. November, 1941 aged 30.
He was the son of Ernest and Florence J. Smith, of Port Talbot; husband of Florence Ellen Smith, of Hayes.
He died at the Military Hospital, Bovingdon Camp, Dorset of injuries sustained when he was thrown from his motor cycle after hitting a brick pillar. At the time he was living at Newlands, Blandford Forum, Dorset.
He is buried at Port Talbot (Holy Cross) Churchyard, Glamorgan. Row 23. Grave 24, and commemorated at St. Mary's, Hayes.

SMITH George Frederick
Stoker D/KX 164962 H.M.S. *Fishguard,* Royal Navy, who died on Sunday, 19rh. November, 1944 aged 19.
He was the son of Sophie Smith, of Hayes.
The *Fishguard* was the ex-United States Coast Guard Cutter *Tahoe* of 1500 tons built in 1927. She survived the war and was returned to the U.S.A. in 1946. All his Death Certificate states is that "he died on war service".
He is buried at Durban (Stellawood) Cemetery, Kwazulu, Natal. South Africa. Block F. Grave 474.. and commemorated at St. Mary's, Hayes.

SMITH John Cameron
Trooper 404018 Warwickshire Yeomanry, Royal Armoured Corps, who died on Monday, 8th. January, 1945 aged 21.
He was the husband of Florence B. Smith, of Berwick Avenue, Hayes.

He died of pulmonary tuberculosis at Twickenham Road, Isleworth. He had been demobilised and was working as a bus conductor.
He is buried at Greenford Park Cemetery, Middx. Sec. S. 16. Grave 24287

SMITH Joseph John
Private S/265454, 208 Petrol Depot, Royal Army Service Corps, who died on Monday, 14th. May, 1945 aged 40.
He was the son of Joseph and Alice Smith of 1, Frogmore Avenue, Hayes; husband of Elsie Winifred Smith, of Hayes.
After the fall of Singapore, the Japanese invaded Java and Joseph was taken prisoner on the 9th. March, 1942. He probably died from malnutrition and disease caused by the terrible conditions in which the Japanese P.O.W. s had to endure.
He is buried at Jakarta War Cemetery, Indonesia. Grave 1. C. 14.

SMITH William Charles
Sergeant 1508018 2nd. Battalion, Monmouthshire Regiment, who died on Saturday, 19th. August, 1944 aged 26.
He was the son of John and Sarah Smith; husband of Doreen Smith, of Hayes.
The 2nd. Battalion was part of the 169th. Infantry Brigade of the 53rd. Welsh Infantry Division who had landed in Normandy on the 27th. June, 1944. He died in the heavy fighting as the Allies tried to close the Gap at Falaise and prevent the Germans escaping to Belgium and Holland. The battle ended on the 22nd. August, and although most of the Germans escaped, they left all their vehicles and equipment behind.
He is buried at Banneville -La-Campagne War Cemetery, Normandy, Grave XV11. A. 3, and commemorated at St. Mary's, Hayes, and St. Peter's and St. Paul's, Harlington

SNELLING Joseph
Sapper 1919918 210 Field Company, Royal Engineers, who died on Thursday, 5th. October, 1944 aged 32.
He was the husband of Norah Snelling, of Hayes.
After the failure of Operation Market-Garden, the airborne assault on Arnhem, on the 25th. September, 1944, Nijmegen became a front line town until February, 1945 and Germans made several counter-attacks from the east. Joseph died of his wounds as a result of one of these attacks, in the No. 3 Casualty Clearing station which was situated in a wooden area known as the Jonkers Bosch in the south-west part of the town.
He is buried at Jonkerbos War Cemetery, Gelderland, Holland. Grave 9. G. 3.

SPENCER Peter John
Pilot Officer 158319 R.A.F.V.R. who died on Wednesday, 1st. December, 1943 aged 20.
He was the son of William V. and Daisy B. Spencer, of Hayes.
He was a pilot flying Spitfire Mark X1 s with 542 Squadron based at Benson, Oxon. They were a photo reconnaissance Squadron and he died in a flying accident. Benson was chosen as the main photo reconnaissance base because of its proximity to the Government in London and Bomber Command Headquarters near High Wycombe, but most of the photos were taken to R.A.F. Medmenham, nr. Marlow for interpretation first.
He is buried at Oxford (Botley) Cemetery, Oxon. Plot 1/2. Grave 120A.

SPRAKE H.W.
Although commemorated at St. Mary's, Hayes, unfortunately I have not been able to trace this person

SQUIBB Charles James
Sergeant 1283565 R.A.F.V.R. who died on Saturday, 20th. September, 1941 aged 25.
He was the son of John W. J. and Sarah Squibb; husband of Iris Maude Squibb, of Bedfont, Middx.
He was flying Spitfire Vb s with 602 Squadron based at Kenley, Surrey. They had taken off on a *circus* over Northern France. A *circus* was a sortie by bombers heavily escorted by fighters, to bring enemy fighters into combat. It was hoped that in 1941 it would ensure that the German retained large numbers of their aircraft in France and did not send them to the Russian front. The aeroplane losses were heavy and as our aircraft were lost over enemy territory the loss of aircrew was also heavy. But it did give our aircrew valuable experience.
Charles failed to return from this operation as did his Squadron colleague Sgt. W. L. Brown.
He is commemorated on the Runnymede Memorial, Panel 52, and at St. Mary's, Hayes, and St. Peter's and St. Paul's, Harlington.

STACE William Charles
Serjeant 6279242 8th. Battalion, Queen's Own Royal West Kent Regiment, who died on Thursday, 3rd. December, 1942 aged 42.
He was the son of William and Sarah Stace; husband of Nellie Kathleen Stace, of Hayes.
He was one of the Guards at a large Italian prisoner-of-war camp at Eldoret which had been established in 1941 when the Italians surrendered in Abyssinia.
He died of heart failure following a stroke.
He is buried at Eldoret Cemetery, Kenya. Grave 257. Eldoret is a town 335 kms. north-west of Nairobi.

STAPLES George Frederick MBE
Warrant Officer 331523 R.A.F. who died on Thursday, 4th. November, 1943.
He was stationed at RAF Odiham, Hants. He was admitted to Park Prewett EMS Hospital on the 3rd. November and died the next day of natural causes.
He is buried at Hayes and Harlington (Cherry Lane) Cemetery, Sec C.2. Grave G. 11.

STEVENS George
Private 14684253 2nd. Battalion, Seaforth Highlanders, who died on Wednesday, 28th. June, 1944 aged 19.
He was the son of Francis L. and Lily R. Stevens, of Hayes.
The 2nd Seaforths was part of the 152nd. Brigade of the 51st. (Highland) Infantry Division. They landed in Normandy as part of the second wave on D-Day and at 8 p.m. were at Ranville 4 miles inland. They then took part in the various attempts to expand the beachhead and capture Caen.
George died at Ste. Honorine, which is between Ranville and the river Caen, from the heavy shelling of the Germans.
In view of his age he must have been a replacement when the Division returned to England in early 1944. He would have been joining men who had fought from Egypt to Tunisia, invaded Sicily and Italy, and who were regarded as crack troops. In fact they were very tired and battle weary, and were being asked to do too much. *Montgomery* had to be very brutal and dismiss some of their senior officers.
He is buried at Hermanville War Cemetery, Calvados. Grave 1. T. 15.

STEVENS William Henry
Leading Aircraftman 1069427 R.A.F.V.R. who died on Wednesday, 14th. July, 1943 aged 32.
He was the son of Reginald and Louisa Stevens, of Walthamstow; husband of Gladys Irene Stevens, of 3, Hollywood Gardens, Hayes. In civilian life he was a clerk.
He was serving at the R.A.F. Station Selectar on Singapore Island but moved to Java where he was captured by the Japanese in early 1942. He was sent to work on the notorious Burma-Siam railway and died of malaria.
He is buried at Kanchanaburi War Cemetery, Thailand. Grave 8. D. 62.
See after **BALL W. F.** for note on Burma-Siam Railway.

STEVENSON Willis
Private 4798784 2nd. Battalion, Lincolnshire Regiment, who died on Saturday, 1st. June, 1940 aged 31.
He was the son of William and Ethel Stevenson; husband of Merle Stevenson, of Hayes.
The 2nd. Battalion was part of the 9th. Infantry Brigade of the 3rd. Infantry Division. The German *Blitzkrieg* had started on the 10th. May and they had advanced rapidly through Belgium and Holland. The Division had fought bravely to hold the line at the Ypres canal but were forced to withdraw to the beaches at Dunkirk. Although the evacuation continued for a few more days, he died in the final day of the evacuation of British troops.
He is commemorated on the Dunkirk Memorial, Nord, France. Column 45.

STOCKER George Henry
Rifleman 6920433 2nd. Battalion, Rifle Brigade, who died on Monday, 26th. October, 1942 aged 29.
He was the son of Charles and Eliza Stocker; husband of Emily Elizabeth Stocker, of Hayes.
The 2nd. Battalion was part of the 7th. Motor Brigade, the mechanised infantry of the 7th. Armoured Division (The Desert Rats). The division was taking part in the diversionary attack in the south of the Alamein line (see note after John **PEACOCK**).
George died on the second day of the battle before *Montgomery* cancelled this attack as it was costing too many casualties.
He is buried at El Alamein War Cemetery, Egypt. Grave XXV1. G. 3.

STOKES William James
Private 14818533 1st. Battalion, The Queen's Royal Regiment (West Surrey), who died on Thursday, 6th, September, 1945 aged 20.
He was the son of Frederick W. and Alice M. Stokes, of Hayes.
The 1st. Battalion was part of the 33rd. Indian Infantry Brigade of the 7th. Indian Infantry Division who had taken part in the recapture of Burma. Now the Japanese had surrendered some of the troops were being sent back to India. William died when his aircraft crashed on the journey.
He is commemorated on the Rangoon Memorial, Burma.(now Myanmar) Face 4. and at St. Mary's, Hayes.

STRONG George
Flight Sergeant 1611982 R.A.F.V.R. who died on Sunday, 25th. February, 1945 aged 30.
He was the son of Joseph and Mary Ann Strong, of Hayes.
He was a Flight Engineer flying Halifax 111 s with 96 Squadron based at Leconfield, Yorks. With the end of the war in sight they were converting from bombers to transports. He died in a flying accident when his aircraft crashed at 1535 hrs. 300 yards west of Brantingham Church, Yorks. (a few miles west of Hull.
He is buried at Beverley (Queensgate) Cemetery Yorks. Block 73 Grave 18.

SUTCLIFFE Jack
Sergeant 1324374 R.A.F.V.R. who died on Sunday, 20th. June, 1943 aged 22.
He was a rear gunner flying Halifax 11 s with 10 Squadron of 4 Group based at Melbourne, Yorks.
They took off at 2215 hrs. to attack the Schneider Armament Works at Le Creusot and were shot
down over France. All seven of the crew were killed and are buried at Bretteville-Sur-Laize
Canadian War Cemetery, Calvados. Collective Grave XX1V. D. 1-4. He is commemorated at St.
Mary's, Hayes.
290 aircraft were despatched, the bombing was fairly successful, and only 2 Halifaxes were lost.

SWANN Kenneth Robert
Pilot Officer R.A.F.V.R. who died on Tuesday 14th. October, 1941 aged 26.
He was the son of Thomas and Rachel E. Strong, of Holt, Norfolk.
He was a Wireless Operator / Air gunner flying Hudson Mk. 1 twin engined bomber/anti-submarine
aircraft with 6 Operational Training Unit based at Thornaby, North Yorkshire when his aircraft
crashed at 2130 hrs. near Nunthorpe, Yorks.
He is buried at Holt Burial Ground, Grave D. 839, and commemorated at St. Peter's and St. Paul's,
Harlington.

SWEETING Charles Robson
Sub-Lieutenant (Air) H.M.S. *Saker*, Royal Naval Volunteer Reserve, who died on Saturday, 17th.
February, 1945 aged 19.
He was the son of H. and Minerva Sweeting, of Hayes.
H.M.S. *Saker* was an American Air Station in Brunswick, Maine leased to the Fleet Air Arm and
Charles was there with 1835 Squadron converting to Chance-Vought Corsairs 1V s, a powerful
single-engined fighter bomber with gull wings. He was flying from Floyd Bennett Field in New
York (where he had probably been on leave) to Brunswick when his aircraft, a Gruman Goose, a
twin-engined amphibious aircraft crashed into Long Island Sound. Charles and three of his
comrades were killed.
He is buried at Long Island National Cemetery, Farmingdale, New York. Post Sec. Grave 25510,
and commemorated at St. Mary's Hayes

TALLACK Frederick Harry
Private 3133279 5/7th. Battalion, Gordon Highlanders. who died on Monday, 5th. April, 1943.
He was the husband of Katie Nellie Tallack of Hayes.
The 5/7th. Gordons was part of the 27th. Infantry Brigade of the 51st. Highland Infantry Division
which had advanced from El Alamein to Tunisia and were now fighting the final battles in North
Africa.
The last defensive line before Tunis was at Wadi Akarit (Wadi is a dried up riverbed) and the two
Gordon Highlander battalions were sent forward to contact the enemy some 2000 yards from the
Wadi. Frederick was wounded in these early encounters and died on the 5th. The Divisional
Intelligence summary stated:-
"There is no doubt that this was the fiercest fighting the Division had experienced in the campaign"
They continued to advance and occupied the town of Sfax on the 10th. The Division went into
reserve and the end came in North Africa when the Axis surrendered on 7th. May and Tunis was
occupied.
He is buried at Sfax War Cemetery, Tunisia. Grave VI. B. 17. Sfax is 270 kms. south of Tunis.

TAPLIN William Harry
Gunner 6214942, 72 Anti-Tank Regiment, Royal Artillery, who died on Saturday, 19th. December, 1942 aged 27.
He was the son of Charles G. and Nellie R. Taplin; husband of Mary Evelyn Violet Taplin, of Bedfont, Middx.
The invasion of North Africa (Operation *Torch*) began on the 8th. November, 1942 with the Allies landing at Algiers, Oran and Casablanca. The 72 Regiment was part of the 6th. Armoured Division which landed as follow-up troops on the 28th. Unusually for an Armoured Division it consisted of two infantry brigades and only one armoured.
He died in the fighting during the attempt of the Allies to reach Tunis before the end of 1942. The Germans had reacted too quickly and rushed troops into Tunisia from Europe.
He is buried at Medjez-el-Bab War Cemetery, Tunisia. Grave 15. G. 3. Medjez is 60 kms. west of Tunis. He is commemorated at St. Peter's and St. Paul's, Harlington

TAYLOR Alec
Private 6207790 1st. Battalion, Middlesex Regiment, who died on the Friday, 2nd., October 1942 aged 21.
He was the son of Robert E. and Hettie A. Taylor, of Harlington.
He was taken prisoner at Hong Kong and died on the Japanese *Lisbon Maru* being transported to Japan
Please see Ronald **BATH** for the full details,
He is commemorated the Sai Wan Memorial, Hong Kong. Column 16., and at St. Mary's, Hayes.

TAYLOR Arthur John
Police Constable who died on Friday, 17th. April, 1941, aged 28 following an air raid on Paddington Station.
He was the son of Mr. and Mrs. E. Taylor of 42, Stratford Road, Southall; husband of Phyllis Elizabeth Taylor, of 22, Barnhill, Road, Yeading Lane, Hayes.

TAYLOR Robert Jackson
Private 3604592 4th. Battalion, Border Regiment, who died on Saturday, 20th. May, 1944 aged 30.
He was the son of Lancelot and Margaret J. Taylor; husband of Josie Jane Taylor, of Hayes.
In Burma in the early months of 1944 the whole situation was about to change very rapidly. The Allies, after the long retreat of 1942 were attacking in the Arakan, and had at last worked out the tactics to defeat the Japanese. They no longer maintained a front line but fought in rectangles, thus defeating the Japanese tactics of carrying out a left hook and establishing a road block behind the Allied troops. They then stayed put, relied on all round defence and as they had complete air supremacy could be supplied from the air. The 2nd. Offensive had begun in November 1943 in the Arakan, and despite a Japanese offensive they had cleared it of them by the 3rd.May.

The Chindits
The *Chindits* (Burmese for Lions) operated behind enemy lines; their main difference from S.O.E. and the Commandos was that they operated in considerable force, sometimes as many as three or five brigades each of 3000 men. They were airlifted, mainly in gliders, into Northern Burma and caused havoc to the Japanese. They were commanded by *Orde Wingate* who had the complete support of *Churchill*, but General *Slim* had his reservations about the their achievements because they were crack troops, and they suffered heavy casualties. *Slim* did not believe in private armies.

Operation "*Thursday*" was launched in early 1944 and was the plan to insert six brigades into Northern Burma and with the Chinese to draw the Japanese troops away from the Arakan so the Allied forces could advance along the coast.

The Japanese however had decided to try and take the Plain of Imphal, and advance northwards to Dinapur, the rail junction for India and use this as a springboard for the invasion of India. They also sent a force northwards to seize the hill-top station of Kohima and block the road from India to Imphal. General *Slim* now decided to withdraw the Allied forces to the plain of Imphal, thus concentrating his forces and lengthening the Japanese lines if communication. He also decided to reduce the Chindit force by half, and use three brigades to help with the defence of Kohima and Imphal.

The 4th. Battalion Border Regiment together with 3rd. Duke of Wellingtons and the 1st. Essex formed the 23rd. Infantry Brigade (6th. Chindits) were now transferred to help the 2nd British Infantry Division raise the siege of Kohima. Now took place what was probably the heaviest fighting of WW2 and they broke through to Kohima on the 2nd. April, but it was not until the 16th. May that the last Japanese troops were cleared from the Kohima Ridge. The Japanese would not withdraw and Robert died in the later fighting. It was not until the 22nd. June that the road from Kohima to Imphal was opened, but they had survived because of the air drops of supplies.

If 23 Brigade had gone with the Chindits they would have suffered the same very heavy casualties of the three Brigades involved, for what was unfortunately limited results

He is buried at Kohima War Cemetery, Grave 3. D. 16.

The Kohima Memorial is dedicated to the 2nd.British Infantry Division.

KOHIMA MEMORIAL
When you go home,
Tell them of us and say,
For your tomorrows.
We gave our todays.

THOMAS Cyril
Donkeyman S.S. *Fort Mumford*, Merchant Navy, who died on Saturday, 20th. March, 1943 aged 41. He was the son of Daniel and Catherine A. Thomas, of Hayes End.

The *Fort Mumford*, was a steamship of 7,100 tons, built in 1942 with a speed of eleven knots. She was torpedoed and sunk by the Japanese submarine I - 27 (*Fukumura*), about 500 miles north west of Ceylon. Her entire crew of 46 and four of the five gunners were lost. Wreckage of her was found on the shore near Cape Comorin.

He is commemorated on the Tower Hill Memorial Panel 51.

It was the I - 27 commanded by *Fukumura* which sank the liner *Khedive Ismail*, of 7,500 tons displacement, off the Maldive Isles in February 1944. Over 1,200 people lost their lives, amongst whom was Kenneth Dowsett, a Royal Artillery Gunner, of Otterfield Road, Yiewsley.

THOMAS Elizabeth Ann
Corporal W/98527 Attached 1 (M) Anti-Aircraft Regiment, Royal Artillery, who died on Thursday, 29th. June, 1944 aged 38.

She was the daughter of Walter D. and Sarah A. Bowen, of Hayes; wife of Charles Thomas, of Winterbourne, Glos.

Elizabeth died "due to war Operations" at Gun Park, Anerley, Penge, Beckenham, Kent.(Probably killed by a V.1. Flying Bomb.)

She is buried at Hayes and Harlington (Cherry Lane) Cemetery, Sec. G.1. Grave N.14

THOMAS Sidney Colin
Leading Cook LT/MX 87588 H.M.S. *Maaloy*, Royal Naval Patrol Service, who died on Monday, 27th. March, 1944 aged 24.
He was the son of Samuel and Edith Thomas, of Regents Park, London.
H.M.S. *Maaloy* was a whaler displacing 249 tons requisitioned by the Admiralty from its owners. It was torpedoed and sunk by the U. 510 (commander Eick) off Ceylon.
He is commemorated on the Lowestoft Naval Memorial, Panel 16. Column 1, St. Mary's. Hayes, and at St. Peter's and St. Paul's, Harlington.

THOMAS William Earl
Sergeant !319646 R.A.F.V.R. who died on Tuesday, 30th. June, 1942 aged 20.
He was the son of William E. and Nellie M. Thomas, of Hayes.
He was a Rear Gunner flying Stirling 1 s with 149 Squadron of 3 Group based at Lakenheath, Suffolk. They took off at 0025 hrs. to attack Bremen, and were shot down by a nightfighter and crashed into the Ijsselmeer, south of Hoorn. All of the crew of seven were killed and are buried at Amsterdam New Eastern Cemetery, Noord-Holland. Plot 69 Row E. Joint Grave 2. He is commemorated at St. Mary's, Hayes.
This was the third attack of the week on Bremen. 258 aircraft were despatched and 11 failed to return. Both the Focke-Wulf factory and the A.G. Weser U Boat construction yard were hit.

THOMPSON Leslie William
Able Seaman C/JX 392378 H.M. Submarine *Stratagem*, Royal Navy, who died on Wednesday 22nd. November, 1944 aged 21.
He was the son of Francis H. and Gertrude E. Thompson, of Hayes.
H.M.S. *Stratagem* was an S Class submarine built in 1943. On patrol in the Malacca Strait on the 18th. November she attacked a Japanese convoy and sank the tanker *Nichinan Maru*. She cleared the area. and about 3 miles from Malacca she was sighted by an aircraft and was then attacked by a destroyer. Undoubtedly the aircraft had spotted the submarine in the clear blue water and called for reinforcements. Alternatively, the aircraft may have been one on the few Japanese aircraft fitted with Magnetic Anomaly Detectors. Just after 1210 hrs. the destroyer delivered two depth-charge attacks which wrecked the submarine's lighting, and damaged the pressure hull. Water was soon pouring into the boat, but although the torpedo officer and thirteen ratings were able to survive in the fore ends, all other compartments were flooded.
Since it was impossible to isolate the fore ends, owing to the flood of water coming through the door, they decided to try an ad hoc escape. They succeeded in blowing a hatch open and ten or the fourteen men in the compartment managed to escape from the ship, but only eight survived the ascent to the surface, to be picked up by the Japanese destroyer. They began a nine month captivity and five died, with only three members of the crew surviving at the end of the war.
Leslie died with the ship and he is commemorated on the Chatham Naval Memorial. Panel 76. 1.

TIMMS Henry
Fire Guard who died on Wednesday, 19th. February, 1944 aged 53.
He was the husband of Annie Timms, of 10, Drenon Square. He was injured in the incident at Longmead Road, and died at Hillingdon County Hospital. He is commemorated at St. Mary's, Hayes.
Please see Charles **DEAMER** for the full details.

TOD William
Lance Serjeant 322280 2nd. Battalion, Highland Light Infantry (City of Glasgow Regiment), who
died on Tuesday, 27th. March, 1945 aged 22.
The Highland Light Infantry was the divisional troops of Eighth Army. The Allies had gone on the
defensive in Spring 1945, due to manpower shortages caused by the civil war in Greece, and William
died in a rare German attack They were waiting to start their final offensive in Italy in April, which
led to the German surrender of all their forces in May.
He is buried at Florence War Cemetery, Italy. Grave IX. J. 3.

TOPHAM Lydon Kenneth
Sergeant 141910 R.A.F.V.R. who died on Sunday, 20th. February, 1944 aged 21.
He was an Air Bomber flying Lancaster 1 s with 463 Squadron of 5 Group based at Waddington,
Lincs. They took off at 2320 hrs. to attack Leipzig and were lost without trace. All the crew of
seven are commemorated on the Runnymede Memorial Panel 239.
823 aircraft were sent that night and 78 failed to return. This was an unhappy raid for Bomber
Command as the German controllers were not mislead by the Kiel Minelaying diversion. As soon
as they crossed the Dutch coast they were met by all the German nightfighter force. The bomber
stream was under attack all the way to the target, and Leipzig was a long penetration for our
bombers. The bombing was concentrated but because the U.S. Air Force bombed it next day, it was
not known how much damage was done by Bomber Command.

TUFFIN George Augustus
Gunner 1145720 3 Reserve Medium Regiment, Royal Artillery, who died on Saturday, 24th. August,
1946 aged 33.
He was the son of George S. and Flora Tuffin, of Hayes; husband of Florence E. Tuffin, of
Marlborough Road, Hillingdon Heath, Uxbridge,
In civilian life he was a bricklayer by trade.
He died of natural causes at his home and is buried at Uxbridge (Hillingdon) Cemetery. Row O. D
Grave 7.

TURNER Raymond Reginald
Corporal 14672811 7th Battalion, Somerset Light Infantry, who died on Tuesday, 27th. March, 1945
aged 19.
He was the son of Reginald and Janet Mary Turner; nephew of Sydney R. Gibbs of Belfont, Middx.
The 7th. Somersets with the 5th. Duke of Cornwall Light Infantry, and the 1st. Worcesters formed
the 214th. Independent Infantry Brigade (not part of a division but under the command of 8th.
Corps) They had landed in Normandy on the 24th. June, 1944 (D-Day+18) and had now fought
their way across Europe to the banks of the Rhine. Following a large artillery barrage the crossing
of the Rhine began on the 23rd. March, and the attack was by large airborne forces and troops in
amphibious vehicles. Raymond died four days later securing the East Bank for the follow-up troops.
The end of the war in Europe was to come in the following month.
He is buried at the Reichswald Forest Cemetery, Kleve, Nordrhein-Westfalen, Germany. Grave 56.
D. 10. The cemetery is 5 kms. south-west of Kleve and contains the burials of over 7000
Commonwealth servicemen. He is commemorated at St. Mary's, Hayes and at St. Peter's and St.
Paul's, Harlington

TYSON Frederick Connelly
Private 5440257 3rd. Battalion, Parachute Regiment, Army Air Corps, who died on Friday, 26th. February, 1943 aged 22.
He was the son of Lillie B. Tyson, of Hayes.
Operation *Torch*, the invasion of North Africa began on the 8th. November, 1942. 3rd. Para. was part of the 1st. Parachute Brigade and they were dropped at Bone to capture the airfield, which they successfully did. Bone is 150 miles east of Algiers. This was the first time that a British parachute battalion had been used in action,
They were then transferred to the 6th. Armoured Division on the 28th. January, 1943 and took part in the advance into Tunisia. Frederick died in this fighting. As Massicault is only 25 kms. south-west of the city of Tunis, and the Allies did not reach there until April he was probably operating behind enemy lines.
He is buried at Massicault War Cemetery, Tunisia. Grave III. L. 10.

VAN William Henry
Private 5243496 1st. Battalion, East Surrey Regiment, who died on Monday, 17th. June, 1940 aged 36.
He was the son of William T. and Jane Van; husband of Ethel Maude Van, of Harlington.
The 1st. Battalion was part of the 11th. Brigade of the 4th. Infantry Division who were sent to join the British Expeditionary Force in October 1939. When the Germans attacked on May 10th.through the Ardennes and Belgium they were forced to withdraw. They fought their last major battle defending the Ypres-Comines canal from the 26th. to 28th. May and then the division was evacuated from Dunkirk. The last British troops leaving on the 1st. June. But William died on the 17th. June when all fighting had ceased and he does not have a known grave. It is therefore possible that in the fog of battle the date of his death is not correct.
He is commemorated on the Dunkirk Memorial Column 60, and at St. Peter's and St. Paul's, Harlington.

WAISTELL Joseph Johnstone
Lance Corporal 5115171 1/6th. Battalion The Queen's Royal Regiment (West Surrey), who died on Monday, 13th. March, 1945 aged 33.
He was the son of James and Emily Waistell; husband of Olive M. Waistell, of Darnall, Sheffield.
The 1/6th. Queens was part of the 131st. Infantry Brigade of the 7th. Armoured Division (The Desert Rats) who had landed in Normandy on the 7th. June, 1944 (D-Day+1) and fought their way across France, Belgium, and Holland to the borders of Germany by December 1944. On the 4th. December the battalion was transferred to the 231 Infantry Brigade of the 50th. (Northumberland) Infantry Division.
He died of wounds received in the Battle of the Rhineland which took place from the 8th. February to the 10th. March.
He is buried at Durnbach War Cemetery, Bad Tolz, Bayern, Germany. Grave 3. E. 10. Durnbach became the main burial ground in Germany after the war, and he was reburied there. He is commemorated at St. Mary's, Hayes, and St. Peter's and St. Paul's, Harlington

WALLIS Robert Alexander
Private 5383464 1st. Battalion, Oxford and Bucks Light Infantry, who died on Sunday, 19th. May, 1940 aged 24.
He was the son of Bryce and Amy Wallis, of Hayes.
The 1st. Battalion was part of the 43rd. Brigade of 48th. Infantry Division who were sent to join the British Expeditionary Force in France on the 29th. January, 1940. On May 10th the Germans

launched their Blitzkreig (Lightning War) through the Ardennes, crossing the Meuse and racing towards the Atlantic coast. On May 19th. they had reached Peronne on the Somme and cut the British and French forces in two. Robert died in this battle

He is buried at Isieres Communal Cemetery, Hainaut, Belgium. Collective Grave 1-9.

This is the only Commonwealth War Grave of WW11 in this cemetery and the other casualties buried in this grave are a Captain, 2nd. Lieutenant. and six Other Ranks from the 4th. Cheshires who were the Machine Gun Battalion attached to Central Head Quarters, BEF. After France 1940 the Ox. and Bucks were formed into a crack Airborne/Glider regiment.

WALTON Edward
Signalman LT/JX 187825 H.M.S. *Bedlington*, Royal Naval Patrol, Service, who died on Wednesday, 5th. April, 1944 aged 28.

He was the son of James and Nancy Walton, of Crowland Avenue, Hayes.

He died of bronchial pneumonia at Hillingdon County Hospital, Uxbridge, In civilian life he was a butcher's assistant.

It has not been possible to identify H.M.S. *Bedlington*, but she was probably a shore establishment. because his address is given as 15,????, Chippenham, Wilts.

He is buried at Hayes and Harlington (Cherry Lane) Cemetery, Sec. R.1. Grave N. 4.

WARD Leslie Alonzo
T/14625991 143 Tank Transport Company, Royal Army Service Corps, who died on Thursday, 10th. May, 1945 aged 34.

He was the son of Mr. and Mrs. Peter Ward; husband of Phyllis Doreen Ward, of Hayes.

As Admiral *Doenitz* surrendered to Field-Marshall Montgomery on May 4th.at Luneberg Heath, he was probably one of the last British soldiers to die in battle in Europe, but I have not been able to locate the exact position.

He is buried at Becklingen War Cemetery, Soltau, Niedersachsen, Germany. Grave 5. B. 11. This cemetery, overlooks Luneberg Heath and contains 2374 WW11 casualties brought in from the surrounding area.

WATERS Edgar Henry William
Chief Engine Room Artificer D/M 6006 H.M.S. *Courageous*, Royal Navy, who died on Sunday, 17th. September, 1939 aged 43.

He was the son of Harry and Kate Waters; husband of Kathleen Mary Waters, of Hayes.

H.M.S. *Courageous* an aircraft carrier of 22500 tons was torpedoed south-west of Ireland by German submarine *U.29* at 2000 hours and sank in less than 15 minutes. 518 men were lost and there were 742 survivors. After covering the passage of the BEF to France, *Courageous* was being employed in anti-submarine operations in the Western Approaches. Using the *Courageous* on this type of operation was considered by most historians to be most ill-advised.

He is commemorated on the Plymouth Naval Memorial,. Panel 34. Column 1.

Kindly note **Robert T. Cooper** of Eastcote also died in this ship.

WATTS Charles Henry
Private 14972542 2nd. Battalion, Royal Scots, who died on Sunday, 13th. April, 1947 aged 20.

He was the son of George H. and Winifred M. Watts, of 125, Minet Drive, Hayes.

He died of pulmonary tuberculosis at the Harefield County Hospital, Harefield.

He is buried at Hayes (St. Mary's) Churchyard.

WATTS Ernest Reginald
Flight Sergeant 1388097 R.A.F.V.R. who died on Thursday, 11th. November, 1943 aged 23.
He was the husband of Ada Elizabeth Watts, of Hayes.
He was a navigator flying single engined Lysander 111 Army Co-operation aircraft with 161
Squadron based at Tempsford, Beds. Tempsford was the main airfield used by the Special
Operations Executive (S. O. E). This organisation had been founded by *Winston Churchill* after the
fall of France in 1940 with the words "Now go and set Europe aflame"
Their object was to help the Resistance with spies, arms and all available means, ready for the return
of the Allies to the Continent, They took off that night for France, crashed and the three crew are
buried at St. Desir War Cemetery, Calvados, France. Collective grave VII A. 2-5. Ernest is
commemorated at St. Mary's, Hayes.

WAYE Reginald Frederick Dennis   DSM
Leading Telegraphist C/JX 137731 H.M. Submarine *Triumph*, Royal Navy, who died on Tuesday,
20th. January, 1942 aged 24.
He was the son of Richard and Constance Mabel Waye, of Hayes.
The *Triumph* was a T Class submarine built at Barrow in 1938. She was regarded as a "lucky"
submarine, because in December 1939 a drifting mine in the Skagerrak had blown off her bows but
she had managed to return to port.
She departed from Alexandria on the 26th. and landed a Special Operations party near Bierans on
the 30th. Their orders were to continue the patrol in the Aegean and rescue a party of POW s on the
9th. January, but she failed to make the rendezvous, and nothing more was heard from her. It was
therefore presumed she was mined some time after the 30th in the area off Hydra. There were no
survivors of the crew of 53.
He is commemorated on the Chatham Naval Memorial. Panel 59. 2, and at St. Mary's, Hayes.
The entry in the London Gazette of 5th. April, 1942, states
"He was awarded the Distinguished Service Medal for daring enterprise and devotion to duty whilst
serving in His Majesty's submarines".

WEATHERHEAD Albert John
Ordinary Seaman, P/JX 232439 H.M.S. *Sotra*, Royal Navy, who died on Thursday, 29th. January,
1942 aged 25.
He was the son of Albert E. and Nellie E. Weatherhead, of Hayes.
The *Sotra* was a whaler of 313 tons displacement, built in 1925 and requisitioned by the Admiralty.
She was sunk by Axis aircraft in the Eastern Mediterranean, off Bardia, Libya.
He is commemorated on the Portsmouth Naval Memorial. Panel 66. Column 1. and at St. Mary's,
Hayes.

WEBB Bertram James.
Private 10594472 Pioneer Corps, who died on Tuesday, 17th, September, 1946 aged 37.
He was the son of James and Florence Webb, of Bedfont, Feltham; nephew of Mr. & Mrs. E.A.
Woods, of Fairholm Cottages, Bath Road, Harlington, Hayes.
He died of a perforated ulcer at Hillingdon County Hospital, Uxbridge, In civilian life he was an
aircraft riveter.
He is buried at Bedfont Church Cemetery,.

WEST Alfred Frederick
Leading Aircraftman 1650024 R.A.F.V.R. who died on Thursday, 14th. November, 1946 aged 24.
He was the son of Alfred J. and Lilian M. Ward; husband of Irene Jesse West, of Hayes.
Alfred was serving as a fitter with 35 Wing. He was admitted to 54 R.A.F. Hospital, BAFO on the
26th. June, 1945 seriously ill with anaemia. He was evacuated to R.A.F. Hospital, Wroughton,
Wilts. and transferred to King Edward VII Sanatorium where he died of acute leukaemia.
He is buried at Chingford Mount Cemetery, Essex. Sec. E.6. Grave 46925.

WESTCOTT Eric John
Private 6021770 1/4th. Battalion, Essex Regiment, who died on Saturday, 18th. July, 1942 aged 22.
He was the son of Sydney and Sarah J. Westcott, of Hayes.
The 1/4th. Essex arrived in Egypt on the 10th. June 1942 as the British component of the 5th. Indian
Brigade of the 4th. Indian Infantry Division. On the 21st. June Tobruk had surrendered after the
battle of Gazala and 32,000 Commonwealth soldiers had been taken prisoner.
The Allies now withdrew to the Alamein position on the 28th. June and *Rommel* began his first
attacks on the Allied positions. Eric died in the quiet period when the Germans were waiting for
reinforcements and supplies. The Deutsche Afrika Korps recommenced their offensive on the
Alamein positions on the 31st. August.
He is buried at El Alamein War Cemetery, Egypt. Grave XXV. F.24.

WHARTON Albert Edward
Private 13019463 Pioneer Corps, who died on Saturday, 29th. September, 1945 aged 33.
He was the son of George H. and Hannah Wharton, of The Crescent, Harlington; husband of Emily
Wharton.
He died of tuberculosis at the Hillingdon County Hospital, Uxbridge. In civilian life he was a
General Labourer.
He is buried at Hayes and Harlington (Cherry Lane) Cemetery. Sec. C.2.. Grave J. 34.

WHITE Alfred
Rifleman 5852346 1st. Battalion, Rifle Brigade, who died on Saturday, 20th. January, 1945 aged 28.
He was the son of Reginald and Winifred D. White, of Harlington.
The 1st. Battalion was the infantry arm of the 22nd. Armoured Brigade of the 7th. Armoured
Division (The Desert Rats) who had landed in Normandy on the 7th. June. 1944 D-day +1. They
had fought their way across France, Belgium and Holland and were now ready for the advance to the
west bank of the Rhine in Germany.
The Germans still held a narrow bridgehead west of the river Roer, south of Roermond which is
21kms. south-east of Eindhoven. As a preliminary to his main offensives Operations *Grenade* and
Veritable Montgomery ordered Operation *Blackcock* to be carried out by the Desert Rats and the
52nd. Lowland Infantry Division. They attacked in the familiar sodden winter conditions on the
10th. January. The operation went slowly but by the 28th. January they had achieved success, but
Alfred had died in the middle of the operation. The Germans had been driven east of the Roer but
then they opened the sluices and flooded the valley, causing considerable delay to the Allied
advance.
He is buried at Nederweert War Cemetery, Limburg, Holland. Grave III. F. 2. Nierderwest is a
village is 38 kms. north west of Roermond. He is commemorated at St. Peter's and St. Paul's,
Harlington.

WHITE Alfred
Gunner 1737059 Royal Artillery, who died on Tuesday, 29th. April, 1941 aged 31.
He was the husband of Eleanor Gertrude White, of Wentworth Crescent., Harlington.
He died at Hayes Cottage Hospital, Hayes of shock from a fractured spine and multiple injuries after being hit by a motor bus. In civilian life he was a Nurseryman/Gardener.
He is buried at Hayes and Harlington (Cherry Lane) Cemetery, Sec. C.1. Row R. 10.

WHITE Thomas
Sergeant 926205 R.A.F.V.R. who died on Saturday, 1st. July, 1944.
He was a Flight Engineer flying Lancaster 111 s with 626 Squadron of 1 Group based at Wickenby, Lincs. They took off at 2210 hrs. to attack the railway yards at the small town of Vierzon, south of Orleans. They crashed at Theilay (Loir-et-Cher), a village just to the west of the rail link between Salbris and Vierzon. Four of the crew died including Thomas and are buried at Theilay Communal Cemetery, Loie-et-Cher, Collective grave 1. Two of the crew were captured and made POW s, but one of the airgunners evaded the Germans. 118 aircraft had attacked with great accuracy and 14 were lost.

WHITEFIELD Cyril Franklin
Sergeant 1425903 R.A.F.V.R. who died on Monday, 25th. September, 1944 aged 22.
He was the son of John and Mary Anne Selina Whitefield (nee Smith), of Hayes.
See his brother Leslie below who had been killed in February 1944.
Cyril was a Mid-Upper Air Gunner flying Lancaster 111 s with 463 Squadron of 5 Group based at Waddington, Lincs.
They took off at 1731 hrs. to bomb the strong points at Calais to help the advance of the Canadian Army. They crashed in the target area, and the pilot, rear-gunner and Cyril were killed. The other four crew members parachuted to safety and evaded capture.
He is commemorated on the Runnymede Memorial Panel 240, and at St. Mary's Hayes.
188 aircraft were sent and as the target was obscured by cloud they used sky-markers directed by their *Oboe* radio beam aids. Eight aircraft including Cyril's were lost on this raid.

WHITEFIELD Leslie Wilfred
Sergeant 1253817 R.A.F.V.R. who died on Friday, 25th. February, 1944 aged 27.
He was the brother of Cyril (see above) who was five years younger
He was an Air Bomber flying Lancaster 111 s with 156 Squadron of 8 Group based at Warboys, Hunts. They took off at 1835 hrs. to bomb Schweinfurt, and were shot down over the target area.
All the crew of seven were killed and are buried at Durnbach War Cemetery, Totz, Bayern..
Collective grave 4 K. 2. 7. He is commemorated at St. Mary's, Hayes.
734 aircraft were despatched and it was the first attack by Bomber Command on this centre of German ball bearing manufacture. The Americans had attacked in 1943 in daylight but they incurred horrendous losses (See the film "Twelve O'clock High" starring *Gregory Peck*). One week before this raid, with the decimation of the Luftwaffe and the introduction of the Mustang long range escort they had returned to bomb Schweinfurt.
The R.A.F. Bomber Force was divided into two halves with a two hour time difference. This was rewarded with the loss of only 31 aircraft, which was very satisfactory, considering the distance flown to the target.

WHITTLE John
Serjeant 4451578 Army Catering Corps, attached Royal Artillery who died on Friday, 1st. December, 1944 aged 40.
He was the husband of Mary Whittle, of Hayes.
The Germans had withdrawn from Greece in the Autumn of 1944, leaving a vacuum which was filled by the Communist Resistance ELAS supported by the Russians. They were opposed by the democrats and the monarchists and a fierce civil war was started. British and Indian troops were sent to restore order with the 2nd. Independent Parachute Brigade arriving on the 14th. October, 1944.
John who was attached to the Royal Artillery was a passenger on the *Empire Dace*, a former Townsend Bros. ferry of 700 tons built in 1942. She had a crew of 20 and was carrying 100 passengers when she struck a mine and sank at the entrance to Missolonghi harbour. At least 45 lives were lost, including John.
As he was lost at sea he is commemorated on the Athens Memorial, Face 10.

WILKINS Alfred Lyddite Joffre
Aircraftman 1st. Class 1263588 R.A.F.V.R. who died on Thursday. 8th. June, 1944 aged 28.
He was the son of Alfred and Sarah M. Wilkins; husband of Ethel Gladys Wilkins, of Hayes.
He was employed as a driver with 6570 Servicing Echelon. He was dangerously injured in a road traffic accident on D-Day. He was admitted to the Radcliffe Hospital, Oxford and died of his injuries.
He is buried at Harwell Cemetery, Berks. Grave 554.

WILLIS Frederick William
He was a civilian, aged 49 and the husband of Louisa Willis, of 231, Station Road, Hayes.
He died on Thursday, 1st. May, 1941 in an air raid at the Alexandra Hotel, Knightsbridge, City of Westminster.
He is commemorated at St. Mary's, Hayes, and at St. Peter's and St. Paul's, Harlington.

WILSON Alfred G.L.
Signalman 13096995 Royal Corps of Signals who died on Wednesday, 4th. November, 1942 aged 20.
He was the son of James J. and Olive L. Wilson, of Harlington.
He was serving in the Signals Section of the 6th. Armoured Division who were due to leave the Clyde shortly to take part in Operation *Torch*, the invasion of North Africa. Alfred died in an accident at Fenwick, Kilmarnock, which is south of Glasgow.
He is buried at Hayes and Harlington (Cherry Lane) Cemetery, Sec. C.2. Grave N.24 and is commemorated at St. Mary's, Hayes, and at St. Peter's and St. Paul's, Harlington.

WINTER Cyril Arthur
Sergeant 1614511 R.A.F.V.R. who died on Sunday, 24th. December, 1944 aged 24.
He was the son of Frederick J. and Elizabeth E. Winter, of Harlington; husband of Dorothy J. Winter, of Abingdon, Berks.
He was as Air-gunner with 35 Squadron flying Lancaster 111 s with 35 Squadron of 8 Group based at Graveley, Hunts. They took off at 1535 hrs. to attack Cologne and crashed almost immediately into trees at Paxton. The villages of Little Paxton and Great Paxton are to the WSW and W. of Graveley airfield, but it is not known which of the two villages are indicated in the records. All the crew of seven were killed.

He is buried at Hayes and Harlington (Cherry Lane) Cemetery, Sec. C. 3. Grave C. 17, and is also commemorated at St. Peter's and St. Paul's, Harlington.
97 Lancasters and 5 Mosquitoes were despatched. 5 Lancasters were lost with two, including Cyril's, crashing in England. The *Oboe* marking (radio beam system) and the resultant bombing was extremely accurate. The local report says that the railway tracks were severely damaged, and an ammunition dump destroyed.

WOODGER Roy George
Corporal 2358126 Royal Corps of Signals, who died on Saturday, 6th, December, 1941 aged 30.
He was the son of James and Amy Woodger; husband of Olive May Woodger, of Hayes.
Operation *Crusader* began on the 19th. November, 1941. This was the Eighth Army's offensive from Egypt into Cyrenacia to relieve the besieged Tobruk. This was successfully done and Roy died on the day that *Rommel* decided the battle was lost, and withdrew westward.
He is buried at Tobruk War Cemetery, Libya, Grave 7. M. 11, and commemorated at St. Mary's, Hayes.

WORKMAN Royston Graham
Sergeant 656278 R.A.F.V.R. who died on Tuesday, 10th. November, 1942 aged 25.
He was the son of Theophilus and Ellen Workman; husband of Joan Elsie Workman, of Hayes.
He was a pilot flying Wellington 1 C s with 40 Squadron based at Fayoum Road, just south of Cairo.
He flew into the ground on take-off.
He is buried at Heliopolis War Cemetery, Cairo, Egypt. Grave 3. A. 8.

Hayes, Harlington 1939 - 1945   Lest We Forget

Name	Rank	Force	Command	Unit	Age	Date of Death	Place of Burial	Where Commemorated
Abbott H.T.A. DSM	Lead. Seaman	Royal Navy	H.M.S.Avenger	Aircraft Carrier	39	15.11.1942		Chatham
Abley P.K.	L.A.C.	R.A.F.V.R.	8 Service Flying School	Montrose, Scotland	19	1.11.1940	Merthyr Tydfil, Glam.	
Acourt R.G.	Private	Army	Dorsetshire Regiment	2nd. Battalion	24	20.3.1945	Taukkyan, Burma	
Aldridge W.R.	Gunner	Army	Royal Artillery	191 Herts & Essex Yeo.	19	17.7.1943	Cherry Lane, Harlington	
Andrews C.E.	Craftsman	Army	R.E.M.E. Passenger	S.S. Strathallan	31	22.12.1942	La Reunion, Algeria	
Andrews S.E. DFM	Flying Officer	R.A.F.	Middle East Airforce	No.3 Aircraft Repair Unit	N/K	9.8.1942	Ismailia, Egypt	
Aplin D. P.	Sergeant	R.A.F.V.R.	Bomber Command	57 Squadron	N/K	8.21.1945	Helsingborg, Sweden	
Arnold I.J.	Private	Army	Herts Regiment	2nd. Battalion	24	16.5.1944	Cassino, Italy	
Ashfield E.W.	Corporal	R.A.F.	Army Co-operation	651 Squadron	40	3.11.1942	Giasserton.Wigtownshire	
Ashworth E.W.	2nd. Engineer	Merchant Navy	S.S. River Lugar	Steamship	54	26.6.1941		Tower Hill
Ashworth F.	Sergeant	R.A.F.	24 Elementary Flying School		N/K	24.5.1941	Cherry Lane, Harlington	
Atkins F.	Private	Army	East Surrey Regiment	2nd. Battalion	23	7.2.1942		Singapore
Baber S.E.	Sergeant	R.A.F.V.R.	Bomber Command	166 Squadron	21	31.8.1943		Runnymede
Bacon J.E.	Flt. Sergeant	R.A.F.V.R.	Coastal Command	119 Squadron	22	14.7.1942		Runnymede
Bacon T. J.	Sergeant	R.A.F.V.R.	Middle East Airforce	39 Squadron	26	14.4.1942		Alamein
Baisden A.V.	Gunner	Army	Royal Artillery	1 Airlanding Lt. Regt.	28	24.9.1944	Arnhem, Holland	
Baker A.	Private	Army	West Yorkshire Regt.	1st. Battalion	30	12.3.1944		Rangoon
Baldwin W.C.	Gunner	Army	Royal Artillery	12 Coast Regiment POW	22	1.10.1942		Sai Wan, China
Ball W.F	Gunner	Army	Royal Artillery	118 Field Regiment POW	23	27.6.1943	Kanchanaburi, Siam	
Bamber H.J.	Flight Lieutenant	R.A.F.	R.A.F. Cranwell		51	9.5.1941	Cherry Lane, Harlington	
Banks R.		Unable to trace						
Barker W.C.	Private	Army	Queens West Surreys	1st. Battalion	19	27.7.1945	Brookwood, Surrey	Rangoon, Burma
Barnes F.C.	Corporal	R.A.F.	80 Wing, Windleham		29	18.4.1942	Battersea, London	
Barnes G	Civilian				63	17.4.1941		
Barrow S. F.	Sergeant	R.A.F.V.R.	Bomber Command	166 Squadron	22	26.5.1943	Eindhoven, Holland.	
Baskerville G.D.		Unable to trace						
Bass G.J.	Ord. Seaman	Royal Navy	H.M.S. Culver	Cutter	21	31.1.1942		Portsmouth
Bass R.L.	Ord. Seaman	Royal Navy	H.M.S. Actaeon	Sloop	19	20.12.1946		Portsmouth
Bath R.J.	Private	Army	Middlesex Regiment	1st. Battaluon POW	26	1.10.1942		Sai Wan, China
Baxter J.C. MM	Private	Army	Hampshire Regiment	2/4th. Battaluon	22	18.12.1944		Phaleron, Athens
Baxter M.F.	Flying Officer	R.A.F.V.R.	Bomber Command	10 Squadron	27	22.11.1943		Runnymede
Beale L.L.	Gunner	Army	Royal Artillery	121 Field Regiment	24	14.5.1944	Enfidaville, Tunisia	

Name	Rank	Force	Command	Unit	Age	Date of Death	Place of Burial	Where Commemorated
Beck A.	Private	Army	Kings Own Lancs Regt.	1st. Battalion	30	15.7.1944	Arezzo, Italy	
Beebe K.C.	Gunner	Army	Royal Artillery	25 Field Regiment	20	16.7.1944	St. Manvieu. Caen	
Bennett J.W.R.	Private	Army	Army Air Corps	2nd. S.A.S. Regiment	20	16.10.1944	Durnbach, Bayern	
Benton D.	Lieutenant	Army	Royal Corps of Signals	8th. Army	25	31.3.1945	Ravenna, Italy	
Beyan S.	Fusilier	Army	Royal Welch Fusiliers	1st. Battalion	21	10.5.1940	Lille, France	
Biggs L.V.	Gunner	Army	Royal Artillery	S.S. Strathallan	19	21.12.1942		Brookwood
Binks G.E.	Corporal	Army	Wiltshire Regiment	4th. Battalion	33	10.10.1944	Jonkerbos, Holland	
Birks A.	Fifth. Engineer	Merchant Navy	M.V. Surat		25	6.5.1941		Tower Hill
Blackham P.D.	Flying Officer	R.A.F.V.R.	Bomber Command	9 Squadron	N/K	8.7.1944	Ecqueville, France	
Blackman A.M.	Sister	Army	Queen Alexandra's Impl. Military Nursing Service		28	27.11.1944	Antwerp, Belgium	
Blackwell S.H.	Able Seaman	Royal Navy	H.M.S. Manners	Frigate	19	26.11.1945		Portsmouth
Blease T.H.	Sergeant	R.A.F.	Middle East Airforce	210 Group	N/K	9.12.1943	Algiers	
Bocking R.J.	Sergeant	R.A.F.V.R.	Bomber Command	100 Squadron	20	19.7.1944	Kleve, Germany	
Bodimead E.A.	Driver	Army	R.A.S.C.		20	23.4.1943	Medjez-el-Bab, Tunisia	
Bowgett F.W.	Lance Serjeant	Army	Middlesex Regiment	1st. Battalion	26	9.2.1945	Kleve, Germany	
Brades E.V.	Able Seaman	Royal Navy	H.M.S. Hermes	Aircraft Carrier	18	9.4.1942		Chatham
Breed V.G.	Ord. Seaman	Royal Navy	H.M.S. Hermes	Aircraft Carrier	18	9.4.1942		Chatham
Bryan R.A.E.	Trooper	Army	Royal Armoured Corps	2nd. Derby Yeomanry	21	18.4.1945	Soltau, Germany	
Buckler H.C.J.	Sergeant	R.A.F.V.R.	Bomber Command	166 Squadron	20	3.8.1944	Oise, France	
Bunce R.	Petty Officer	Royal Navy	H.M.S. Firedrake	Destroyer	36	17.12.1942		Chatham
Burrell D.T.	Flight Sergeant	R.A.F.	Middle East Airforce	174 Squadron	20	16.10.1945	Naples, Italy	
Burton J.	Able Seaman	Royal Navy	H.M.S. Isis	Destroyer	19	20.7.1944		Portsmouth
Burton R.H.	Guardsman	Army	Grenadier Guards	1st. Battalion	27	23.9.1944	Uden, Holland	
Campbell W.R	Sergeant	R.A.F.V.R.	Bomber Command	50 Squadron	N/K	30.8.1944	Helsingborg, Sweden	
Canfield E.J.	Ldg.Telegr'phist	Royal Navy	H.M.S. Samphire	Flower class Corvette	42	30.11.1943	Salerno, Italy	
Carbutt C.	Private	Army	Oxford & Bucks Light Inf.	7th. Battalion	N/K	29.9.1943		Chatham
Carey F.H. DSM	Able Seaman	Royal Navy	H.M.S. Firedrake	Destroyer	41	17.12.1942		Chatham
Carpenter R.W.	Sergeant	R.A.F.V.R.	Bomber Command	619 Squadron	N/K	6.11.1944	Poznam, Poland	
Carter J.T.	Staff Sergeant	Army	Royal Electrical & Mechanical Engineers		26	11.3.1944	Cherry Lane, Harlington	
Carter L.J.	Corporal	Army	Royal Army Service Corps		33	13.12.1943	Cherry Lane, Harlington	
Carter L.G.	Gunner	Army	Royal Horse Artillery	5 Regiment	31	15.12.1942		Alamein
Church C.E.	Sergeant	R.A.F.V.R.	Far East Airforce	353 Squadron	24	4.8.1944	Ranchi, India	

Hayes, Harlington 1939 -1945 Lest We Forget.

Name	Rank	Force	Command	Unit	Age	Date of Death	Place of Burial	Where Commemorated
Clare T.	Fusilier	Army	Royal Inskilling Fusiliers	2nd. Battalion	24	13.4.1944	Anzio, Italy	
Clark A.G.	A.C.2.	R.A.F.V.R.	Training	3 Pilots Advanced F.U.	17	24.7.1944	Cherry Lane, Harlington	
Clarke S		Unable to trace						
Coaster K.W.	L.A.C.	R.A.F.V.R.	1 British Flying Training School		19	17.9.1943	Terrell Texas	
Collins R.W.	Marine	Royal Marines	H.M.S. Arethusa	Cruiser	26	18.11.1942		Chatham
Collins R.F.	Artificer 4th Class	Royal Navy	H.M.S. Goodall	Frigate	25	29.4.1945		Chatham
Colton T.C.	Guardsman	Army	Irish Guards	2nd. Battalion	24	1.8.1944		Bayeau
Connell H.A.	Trooper	Army	Royal Armoured Corps	3rd. L'don Sharpshooters	25	2.9.1942	El Alamein	
Cooke C.S.	Petty Officer	Royal Navy	H.M.S. Janus	Destroyer	32	23.11.1944		Portsmouth
Cooper D.L.	Flight Sergeant	R.A.F.V.R.	Middle East Airforce	40 Squadron	21	25.11.1943		Malta
Cooper K.E.	Private	Army	R.A.O.C.	1st. Indian Inf. Bde.	25	5.12.1941		Alamein
Cossom E.E.A.	Private	Army	Durham Light Infantry	9th, Battalion	31	7.6.1944	Bayeau, Normandy	
Coultrup T.	Civilian		Light Rescue Service		42	18.12.1942	Cherry Lane, Harlington	
Cowley J.W.	Corporal	Army	Royal Fusiliers	1st. Battalion	32	5.12.1943	Sangro, Italy	
Cox C.H.	Gunner	Army	Royal Artillery	6th. H.A.A. Regiment	24	2.6.1942	Ranchi, India	
Cripps A.E.	Private	Army	Royal Berkshire Regt.	10th. Battalion	30	7.2.1944	Anzio, Italy	
Cronin R.	Serjeant	Army	East Lancs. Regiment	1st. Battalion	35	7.1.1945	Hotton, Luxemburg	
Crutchfield P.N.	Sergeant	R.A.F.V.R.	Bomber Command	103 Squadron	20	12.5.1944	Antwerp, Belgium	
Curnow F.W.	Gunner	Army	Royal Artillery	138 Field Regiment	19	17.11.1942	Tabarka, Tunisia	
Currie F.	Serjeant	Army	Royal Artillery	87 Lt. A.A. Regiment	35	17.4.1944	Portland, Dorset	
Curtis S.	Driver	Army	R.A.S.C.	718. Airb'ne Lt Comp. Co	24	10.6.1944	Ranville. Calvados	
Cust P.G.	Sergeant	R.A.F.V.R.	Bomber Command	271 Squadron	32	8.2.1943	Brookwood, Surrey	
Daniels G.	L.A.C.	R.A.F.V.R.	Transport Command	271 Squadron	34	15.11.1946	Marseilles, France	
Davis E.J. W.	Flight Sergeant	R.A.F.V.R.	Bomber Command	9 Squadron	24	18.2.1943	Niedersachsen, Germany	
Day F.W.	Warrant Officer	Army	Northamptonshire Regt.	2nd. Battalion	33	19.3.1944	Anzio, Italy	
Day P.	Sergeant	R.A.F.V.R.	Bomber Command	170 Squadron	N/K	7.1.1945	Dunbach, Bayern	
Daykin D.	Quartermaster	Army	Duke of Wellingtons	1st. Battalion	41	7.11.1943	Medjez-el-Bab, Tunisia	
Deamer C	Air Raid Warden		Civilian		47	19.2.1944	Cherry Lane, Harlington	
Dean G.A.			East Yorkshire Regiment	1st. Battalion	32	1.12.1944	Madras. India	
Deane C.	Corporal	Army	Royal Artillery	524 Coast Regiment	21	20.6.1942	Cherry Lane, Harlington	
Dennis A.J.	Gunner	Army	Royal Engineers		30	2.4.1945	Phaleron. Athens	
Dennis R.E.A.	Lance Corporal	Army	Royal Army Service Corps	271 Field Company	23	22.6.1941	Cherry Lane, Harlington	

93

Name	Rank	Force	Command	Unit	Age	Date of Death	Place of Burial	Where Commemorated
Devaney J.I.	Private	Army	Pioneer Corps		25	26.2.1941	Carlisle, Cumbria	
Devenney M.R.	Private	Army	York & Lancaster Regt.	Hallamshire Battalion	18	25.6.1944	Tessel, Normandy	
Dines J.F.	Marine	Royal Marines	H.M.S. Condor	Arbroath Air Station	18	13.5.1943	St. Mary's Hayes	
Dodson A.F.	Sapper	Army	Royal Engineers	723 Artisan Works. Co	22	6.4.1944	Bari, Italy	
Elliott E.L.	Private	Army	Hampshire Regiment	1/4th Battalion	39	16.9.1944	Gradara, Italy	
Elliott W.J.	A.C.2	R.A.F.V.R.	R.A.F. Uxbridge		26	27.10.1941	Uxbridge	
Ellis D.M.		Unable to trace						
Ellis R.H.	Corporal	Army	Black Watch	6th. Battalion	29	9.11.1944	Forli, Italy	
Evans H.E.	Ord. Seaman	Royal Navy	H.M.S. Victory	Shore Base	21	11.5.1941	City of London Cemetery, Essex	
Evans T.	Private	Army	East Surrey Regiment	11th. Battalion	27	26.4.1941	Cherry Lane, Harlington	
Exell H.J.	Fusilier	Army	Royal Fusiliers (London)	8th. Battalion	27	11.3.1944	Padua, Italy	
Farr G.W.	Driver	Army	Royal Electrical & Mechanical Engineers		27	14.4.1943	Enfidaville, Tunisia	
Fell J.A.	Flight Sergeant	R.A.F.V.R.	Bomber Command	106 Squadron	21	6.10.1944		Runnymede
Fetherston H.H.	Sergeant	R.A.F.V.R.	Bomber Command	61 Squadron	25	26.3.1942	Kleve, Germany	
Fisher D.	Serjeant	Army	Shropshire Light Infantry	2nd. Battalion	34	1.3.1945	Kleve, Germany	
Fleming H.V.	Ord. Seaman	Royal Navy	H.M.S. Jaguar	Destroyer	N/K	26.3.1942		Plymouth
Foskett W.J.	Firewatcher	Civilian			20	10.5.1941	Cherry Lane, Harlington	
Fraser R.W.	Sergeant	R.A.F.V.R.	Far East Air Force	159 Squadron	23	3.2.1944	Ranchi, India	
Fripp H.J.	Ord. Seaman	Royal Navy	H.M.S. Achates	Destroyer	N/K	31.12.1942		Chatham
Frogley J.E.	Sergeant	R.A.F.V.R.	Far East Air Force		N/K	5.5.1944	Calcutta, India	
Frost E.R.	Lead. Stoker.	Royal Navy	N.M.S. Odin	Submarine	26	27.6.1940		Portsmouth
Fry L.E.	Lance Corporal	Army	York & Lancs Regiment	Hallamshire Battalion	29	26.9.1944	Antwerp, Belgium	
Fry W.A.	Deck Hand	Merchant Navy	S.S. Royal Crown	Steamship	23	30.11.1940	Lowestoft, Suffolk	
Fuller E.P.	Gunner	Army	Royal Artillery	80 Heavy A.A.Regiment	32	8.11.1943	Salerno, Italy	
Furness J.	Chief Stoker	Royal Navy	H.M.S. Penelope	Light Cruiser	37	18.2.1944		Portsmouth
Gardiner A.J.		Unable to trace						
George E.R.	Leading Airman	Royal Navy	H.M.S. Daedalus	Lee-on-Solent Air Station	22	7.3.1943	Haslar, Hampshire	
Giles D.A.N.	Gunner	Army	Royal Artillery	78th. Medium Regiment	20	30.4.1944	Cassino, Italy	
Giles K.A.R.	L.A.C.	R.A.F.V.R.	Middle East Comms.	Kabrit, Egypt	25	13.9.1945	Cairo, Egypt	
Giles W.S.	Lance Corporal	Army	Scots Guards	2nd. Battalion	18	11.3.1945	Kleve, Germany	
Gillick T.F.	Gunner	Army	Royal Artillery	64 Lt. A. A. Regiment	27	11.4.1941	Kingston, Surrey	
Gleed R.G.	Ord. Seaman	Royal Navy	H.M.B.Y. 2077	Brooklyn Y. Minesweeper	N/K	25.10.1944		Lowestoft

Hayes, Harlington 1939 -1945 Lest We Forget

Name	Rank	Force	Command	Unit	Age	Date of Death	Place of Burial	Where Commemorated
Godfrey A.	Serjeant	Army	Royal Artillery	17 Field Regiment	32	9.8.1943	Catania, Sicily	
Gooch E.J.	Lance Bombier	Army	Royal Horse Artillery	6th. Regiment	28	22.7.1941	St. Mary's Hayes	
Gower H.G.	Marine	Royal Marines	No.42 R.M. Commando		20	23.8.1942	Hanwell, Middx	
Gravell L.	Serjeant	Army	Kings Own Scot Borderer:	2nd. Battalion	26	19.1.1944	Coriano Ridge, Italy	Rangoon, Burma
Gray W.T.	Private	Army	Essex Regiment	1/4th. Battalion	29	7.10.1944		
Green G.F.	Private	Army	Sherwood Foresters POW	1/5th. Battalion	30	12.9.1944		Singapore
Griffiths F.	Petty Officer	Royal Navy	H.M.S. Itchen	Frigate	38	23.9.1943		Plymouth
Griffiths L. DSO	Commander	R.N.R.	H.M.S. Yeoman		43	19.7.1944	Woodford, Essex	
Groves F.	Gunner	Army	Royal Artillery	48 Lt. A.A. Regt. POW	28	7.3.1945		Singapore
Guttridge R.A.	Serjeant	Army	Lincolnshire Regiment	2nd. Battalion	26	14.7.1940	Cirencester, Glos.	
Hackwell W.T	Rifleman	Army	King's Royal Rifle Corps		29	26.5.1940	Calais, France	
Haldane S.J.	Serjeant	R.A.F.	Bomber Command	214 Squadron	19	30.8.1940	Zeihem, Holland	
Hall R.J.	Private	R.A.F.	Hampshire Regiment	1st. Battalion	19	14.6.1944	Calvados, France	
Harcourt V.R.G. DFC	Squadron Ldr.	Army	Bomber Command	139 Squadron	25	21.5.1943	Dieppe, France	
Hardy G.W.	Private	Army	East Surrey Regiment	2nd. Battalion	28	5.2.1942		Singapore
Harper L.S.	Driver	Army	Royal Army Service Corp	63 (Airborne) Comp. Co	29	19.9.1944	Arnhem, Holland	
Harris F.J.D.	Cadet 1st Class		Air Training Corps		18	30.7.1944	Oxford (Botley)	
Harvey D.I.		Unable to trace						
Hathorn R.K.W.	Leadg.Air Fitter	Royal Navy	H.M.S. Goldfinch	Air Station, Takali, Malta	23	5.4.1946	Malta	
Haynes W.G.	Lance Corporal	Army	Herefordshire Regiment	1st. Battalion	28	4.2.1944	Anzio, Italy	
Healy T.V.	Volunteer	Home Guard	Middlesex Regiment	17th. Battalion	45	28.3.1941	Cherry Lane, Harlington	
Hearne H.R.	L.A.C.	R.A.F.V.R.	24 Elementary Fl'g Sch'l	Herts	21	7.7.1941	Cherry Lane, Harlington	
Heron S.	L.A.C.	R.A.F.V.R.	Middle-East Airforce	32 Squadron	22	23.7.1943	Bone, Algeria	
Hickman M.F.A.	Serjeant	Army	Royal Engineers		33	3.3.1943	Tehran, Iran	
Hipsey R.	Serjeant	Army	Poyal Armoured Corps	7th. Queens Own Hussar	28	30.3.1942		Rangoon. Burma
Hoare A.J.	Able Seaman	Royal Navy	H.M.S. Acasta	Destroyer	N/K	9.6.1940		Portsmouth
Holmes K.J.	Serjeant	R.A.F.V.R.	Bomber Command	625 Squadron	N/K	16.3.1945	Dumbach, Munich	
Hopkins D.R.	Gunner	Army	Royal Artillery	124 Heavy A.A.Regiment	21	25.12.1943	Cherry Lane, Harlington	
Horspool W.	Private	Army	Dorsetshire Regiment	4th. Battalion	31	10.7.1944	Bayeaux, France	
Howe A.E	Craftsman	Army	Royal Electrical & Mechanical Enineers		22	30.12.1945	Naples, Italy	
Howell F.J	Gunner	Army	Royal Artillery	30 Field Regiment	21	16.9.1944	Gradara, Italy	
Huckell F.	Fusilier	Army	Royal Fusiliers (London)	2nd. Battalion	27	31.5.1940	West Vlaanderen, Belgium	

Hayes, Harlington 1939 - 1945   Lest We Forget

Name	Rank	Force	Command	Unit	Age	Date of Death	Place of Burial	Where Commemorated
Hunt W.J.	Rifleman	Army	London Rifle Brigade	8th Battaliom	27	29.6.1944	Banneville, Calvados	
Hurst D.A.	Private	Army	Queen's (West Surrey).	1/6th. Battalion	19	3.8.1944	Bayeaux, Calvados	
Hutchinson R.W.	Steward	Royal Navy	H.M.S. Vengeance	Aircraft Carrier	18	17.8.1947	Cherry Lane, Harlington	
Hutchinson W.J.		Unable to trace						
Hutchison J.		Unable to trace						
Ingledow J.H.H.	Gunner	Army	Royal Artillery	585 Indep. H.A.A. Batty	25	17.7.1943	Kettering, Northants	
Inns R.L.	L'ce Bomb'dier	Army	Royal Artillery	72 Anti-Tank Regiment	25	27.8.1944	Arezzo, Italy	
James G.R.	Corporal	Army	East Surrey Regiment	1/6th. Battalion	35	28.5.1940	West Vlaanderen, Belgium	
Jarvis A.A.		Unable to trace						
Johnson H.W.J.	L.A.C	R.A.F.V.R.	Bathurst, Gambia	200 Squadron	22	29.9.1942	Fajara, Gambia	
Jones G.B.	Sergeant	R.A.F.V.R.	Bomber Command	75 Squadron	19	26.8.1944	Durnbach, Bayern	
Joys R.H.	Fusilier	Army	Royal Fusiliers London	1st. Battalion	28	18.06.1944	Assisi. Italy	Cassino
Judd S.	Sapper	Army	Royal Engineers	503 Field Company	29	9.9.1943		
Keene R.E.	Sergeant	R.A.F.V.R.	Bomber Command	No.16 O.T.U.	21	15.11.1943	Middleton Stoney, Oxon	
Keen H.F.	Enginemen	Royal Navy	H.M.B.Y. 2035	Brooklyn Y.Minesweeper	20	5.11.1944	West Vlaanderen, Belgium	
Keriford W.L.	Craftsman	Army	R.E.M.E	21 Beach Recov.Section	24	1.11.1944		Groesbeck, Hollanc
Kelly E.G.	Lance Corporal	Army	Queen's (West Surrey).	14th. Battalion	25	21.12.1940	Gerrards Cross, Bucks	
Kidd E.J.	Cook (S)	Royal Navy	H.M.S. Tunisian	Boom Defence Vessel	N/K	9.7.1942		Portsmouth
Knowles D.W.	Fusilier	Army	Royal Fusiliers (London)	2nd, Battalion	28	13.10.1941	Cherry Lane, Harlington	
Lander H.G.	Sapper	Army	Royal Engineers	276 Field Company	33	5.11.1944	Bergen-op-Zoom, Holland	
Lascelles E.H.	L.A.C	R.A.F.V.R.	6341 Light Warning Unit		34	18.9.1944	Arthem, Holand	
Last S.G.	Private	Army	Royal Norfolk Regiment	1st. Battalion	27	8.7.1944	Douvres, Calvados	
Lauder F.J.	Sergeant	R.A.F.V.R.	Bomber Command	51 Squadron	22	3.5.1943	Hayes St. Mary's	
Lauder G.W	Sergeant	R.A.F.V.R.	Middle East Airforce	454 Squadron	N/K	19.4.1945	Padua Italy	
Law A.	Driver	Army	R.A.S.C.	250 Airborne Lt. Comp	25	25.9.1944		Groesbeck,Holland
Laws G.E.	Lance Corporal	Army	Queens West Surreys	1/6th. Battalion	38	30.9.1942	El Alamein	
Leake W.E.	Flight Sergeant	R.A.F.V.R.	Coastal Command	404 (R.C.A.F.) Squadron	30	13.81944	Ile De Re, France	
Learoyd P.J.	Fusilier	Army	Royal Fusiliers (London)		19	12.6.1947	Munster, Germany	
Lenahan J.D.	Pilot Officer	R.A.F.V.R.	Fighter Command	607 Squadron	20	9.9.1940	Cranbrook. Kent	
Lett M.L.	Lance Corporal	Army	Black Watch	5th. Battalion	19	25.2.1945	Rheinberg, Germany	
Lewis I.W.	Bombardier	Army	Royal Artillery	135 Herts Field Regiment	27	11.2.1942		Kranji, Singapore
Loftus T.W.P.	Rifleman	Army	King's Royal Rifle Corps	2nd. Battalion	19	10.7.1944	Cheux, Calvados	

Name	Rank	Force	Command	Unit	Age	Date of Death	Place of Burial	Where Commemorated
Lydon J.P.	Gunner	Army	Royal Artillery	139 Field Regiment POW	42	6.2.1944	Taukkyan. Burma	
McDiarmid E.A.	Stoker 1st Class	Royal Navy	H.M.S. Lothian		34	6.4.1945		Plymouth
McEntegart J.	Lance Serjeant	Army	South Lancs. Regiment	1st. Battalion	33	6.6.1944	Hermanville, Calvados	
MacKrodt A. V.	Captain	Army	Royal Indian Service Corps		N/K	18.5.1944		Rangoon
McMahon D.	Serjeant	Army	Royal Armoured Corps	2nd.Fife/ForfarYeomanry	36	22.9.1944	Mierlo, Holland	
McNamara E.C.	Lead. Seaman	Royal Navy	H.M.S. Duchess	Destroyer	28	12.9.1939		Chatham
McNamara R.	Sergeant	R.A.F.V.R	Bomber Command	22 O.T.U.	N/K	14.10.1941	Cranford. Middx	
Makin G.	Private	Army	Cheshire Regiment	2nd. Battalion	32	17.6.1944	Bayeaux. France	
Mallett R.S. DFC	Flying Officer	R.A.F.V.R	Bomber Command	141 Squadron	N/K	28.6.1944	Eindhoven, Holland	
Malpas A.C.	Gunner	Army	Royal Artllery	6/3 Maritime Regiment	31	7.11.1942		Chatham
Mansfield N.L.	Telegraphist	Royal Navy	H.M.S. Sultan	Singapore Naval Base	20	16.2.1942		Plymouth
Martin F.		Unable to trace						
Mason A.J.C.	Flight Sergeant	R.A.F.V.R.	Bomber Command	103 Squadron	30	16.2.1943	Lorient. France	
Mason R.	A.C.2	R.A.F.V.R.	11 Recruits Centre	Skegness, Lincs.	18	24.10.1942	Southall. Middx.	
Matthew J.P.	Lieut-Commander	Royal Navy	H.M.S. Mersey	No. 6 Depot Liverpool	52	28.7.1942	Hanwell. Middx.	
Mathews J.R.G.	Flight Sergeant	R.A.F.V.R.	Bomber Command	466 Squadron	N/K	20.12.1943	Rheinberg, Germany	
Maxfield F.	Pilot Officer	R.A.F.V.R.	Bomber Command	150 Squadron	29	15.10.1942	Ulrum, Gronigen, Holland	
Mayhew N.K.	Able Seaman	Royal Navy	H.M.S. Eclipse	Destroyer	20	24.10.1943		Portsmouth
Meaby E.P.	Stoker 1st Class	Royal Navy	H.M.L.C.T 839	Landing Ship Tank	N/K	2.11.1944	Ostend, Belgium	
Melville A.	Private	Army	Northants Regiment	2nd. Battalion	28	23.5.1940	Arras. France	
Micklewright F.H.	Civilian				34	19.2.1944	Cherry Lane, Harlington	
Mills W.D.	Flight Sergeant	R.A.F.V.R.	Bomber Command	218 Squadron	23	27.5.1943		Runnymede
Mittell P	Sub-Lieut. (Air)	R.N.V.R.	H.M.S. Heron	Yeovilton, Somerset	23	23.3.1941	St. Columb Major, Cornwall	
Moore R.H.	Warrant Officer	Army	Royal Artllery	63 Anti -Tank Regiment	36	11.5.1940	Fulham Cemetery. Surrey.	
Morris F.A.	Sergeant	Army	Wiltshire Regiment	5th. Battalion	25	22.7.1944	Banneville. Calvados	
Morris W.E.	2nd. Lieutenant	Army	General List	Eighth Army	31	9.10.1944	Cairo, Egypt	
Morton E	Warrant Officer	Army	Royal Artillery	119 Lt.A.A. Regiment	29	19.2.1945	Groesbeek, Holland	
Morton E.L.		Unable to trace						
Moudon C.J.	Firewatcher				45	14.3.1944	Cherry Lane. Harlington	
Mullen M.	Co.Q'masrer Serjt	Army	Pioneer Corps		49	22.5.1940	Southend-on-Sea, Essex	
Murray J.L.	Sergeant	R.A.F.V.R.	13 O.T.U,		N/K	4.8.1945		Runnymede
Nash C.A.R.	Private	Army	Somerset Light Infantry	4th. Battalion	26	30.7.1944	Hottot-Les-Baques. Calvados	

Hayes, Harlington 1939 -1945   Lest We Forget.

Name	Force	Rank	Command	Unit	Age	Date of Death	Place of Burial	Where Commemorated
Nash G. W. DFM	Royal Navy	Lead. Seaman	H.M.S. Danube 111	Tug	38	13.10.1940		Chatham
Newton A.J.	R.A.F	Flying Officer	Bomber Command	101 Squadron	29	4.5.1944	St. Desir. Calvados	
Norman J.H.	Army	Private	Shropshire Light Infantry	2nd Battalion	24	22.7.1944	Douvres, Calvados	
Nugent R.H.	R.A.F	L.A.C.	Adv'd Air Striking Force	142 Squadron	35	14.5.1940	Nancy, France	
Oake J.A.	Army	Serjeant	King's Royal Rifle Corps	2nd. Battalion	33	25.5.1947	Hanwell. Middx	
Oake S.	Royal Navy	Ch.Petty Oficer	H.M.S, Redmill	Frigate	37	27.4.1945		Chatham
Ogden FA.T.	Army	Gunner	Royal Artillery	92 Field Regiment	34	7.8.1943	Catania, Sicily	
O'Shea M.	Army	Fusilier	Royal Fusiliers (London)		28	12.5.1947	Cherry Lane, Harlington	
Otter F.A.	Army	Guardsman	Grenadier Guards	5th. Battalion	31	27.1.1944	Anzio, Italy	
Oxley S.J.	R.A.F.	A.C.1	Middle East Airforce	8 Squadron	19	13.9.1941	Maala, Yemen	
Page A.J.	Army	Guardsman	Grenadier Guards	6th. Battalion	24	30.1.1944	Minturno, Italy	
Parish J.E.	R.A.F.V.R.	L.A.C.	Bomber Command	R.A.F. Honington	27	19.8.1940	Honington, Suffolk	
Parker L.G.	Army	Lance Serjeant	Royal Artillery	72 H.A.A. Regiment	33	19.6.1943	Medjez-el-Bab.Tunisia	
Parker T.	Army	Private	Gordon Highlanders	1st. Battalion	27	15.8.1944	Ranville, Calvados	
Parsons G.E.H.	Royal Navy	Leading Cook	H.M.S, Tempest	T class submarine	N/K	23.2.1942	Bari, Italy	
Peacock J.W. DCM MM	Army	Lieutenant	Royal Armoured Corps	11th. Hussars	22	23.10.1942	El Alamein	
Pearson V.	Army	Rifleman	Rifle Brigade	7th. Battalion London	27	31.3.1943	Sfax, Tunisia	
Peggs E.J.	Army	Corporal	Queens West Surreys	2/5th. Battalion	22	2.9.1944	Gradara, Italy	
Penn W.W,	Army	Serjeant	Buffs (Royal East Kents)	2nd. Battalion	26	26.11.1945	Taukkyan, Burma	
Perryman G. S.	Army	Lance Bomb'dier	Royal Artillery	64th. Anti-Tank Regiment	29	15.5.1944	Cassino, Italy	
Pettet C.E.	Royal Navy	Lead, Seaman	H.M.S. Copra	592 L.C.A. Flotilla	24	7.6.1944	Cherry Lane, Harlington	
Phair S.A,	Army	Private	Beds and Herts.Regt.	5th. Battalion POW	25	22.11.1943	Kanchanaburi. Thailand	
Phipps A.R.	R.A.F.V.R.	Sergeant	Transport Command	46 Squadron	20	24.3.1945	Marseilles, France	
Pollard J.C.	R.A.F.V.R.	Flight Sergeant	Coastal Command	618 / 143 Squadrons	N/K	21.2.1944		Runnymede
Pollard L.J.	Army	Sergeant	Royal Artillery		24	12.12.1944	Islington, Middx.	
Portsmouth R.A.	Army	Gunner	Royal Artillery	48 Light A.A. Regt. POW	25	9.7.1945		Singapore
Prince J.C.	R.A.F.V.R.	Pilot Officer	1653 Hvy Conv'sion Unit	Chedburgh, Suffolk	23	30.10.1943		Runnymede
Prior A.H	Army	Lance Bomb'dier	Royal Artillery	90 Lt. A.A. Regiment	38	17.2.1944	Anzio, Italy	
Pryce W.	Army	Sapper	Royal Engineers	238 Field Company	22	8.12.1944	Bologna, Italy	
Rawlings C.W.H.	R.A.F.V.R.	Sergeant	Bomber Command	42 O.T.U.	30	28.3.1943	Cherry Lane, Harlington	
Read G.E.H.C.	Army	Driver	R.A.S.C.	2 Corps. Petrol Park	26	19.3.1940	Fouquieres, Pas de Calais	
Redfern E. A...	R.A.F.V.R.	Flight Sergeant	Fighter Command	242 Squadron	27	17.8.1941	Etaples, Pas de Calais	

Name	Rank	Force	Command	Unit	Age	Date	Place	Where
Rhodes J.C.	Flight Sergeant	R.A.F.V.R.	Middle East Airforce	603 Squadron	23	15.5.1944	Phaleron, Athens	
Richards N.L.	Sergeant	R.A.F.V.R.	Bomber Command	10 O.T.U, Observers	20	27.6.1944	Cherry Lane, Harlington	
Ridout R.	Gunner	Army	Royal Artillery	117 Field Regiment	20	14.4.1942	Netley, Hants	
Rielly G.K.	Private	Army	Queens West Surreys	1/5th. Battalion	18	20.7.1944	Douvres, Calvados	
Rixon P.A.	Private	Army	Buffs (Royal East Kents)	5th. Battalion	27	8.4.1943	Qued Zarga, Tunisia	
Robbins E.E.	Pilot Officer	R.A.F.V.R.	Middle East Airforce	233 Squadron	22	8.11.1942		Malta
Roberts C.W.	Trooper	Army	Royal Armoured Corps	2nd. Dragoon Guards	21	24.10.1942		Alamein
Roberts R.F.	Flight Sergeant	R.A.F.V.R.	Bomber Command	102 Squadron	22	24.8.1943		Runnymede
Rodden J.A.	Corporal	Army	Royal Ulster Rifles	2nd. Battalion	33	5.8.1943	Catania, Sicily	
Rogers E.F.	Sergeant	R.A.F.V.R.	Middle East Airforce	216 Group	21	2.8.1945	Ramleh, Israel	
Rolfe L.G.	Trooper	Army	Royal Horse Guards	Household Cavalry	18	3.11.1945	Cologne, Germany	
Rolfe R.J.	Sergeant	R.A.F.V.R.	Bomber Command	15 Squadron	21	15.6.1944	Fecamp, Nr. Le Havre	
Rowley G.W.	L.A.C.	R.A.F.V.R.	Middle East Airforce	239 Wing	N/K	29.11.1944	Ancona, Italy	
Russell E.C.T.	Signalman	Army	Royal Corps of Signals	4th. Armoured Brigade	22	11.7.1944	Cheux, Calvados	
Russell F.A.	Private	Army	Devonshire Regiment	12th. Airborne Battalion	28	26.8.1944	St Desir, Calvados	
Salter K.W.	Private	Army	Royal Army Ordnance Corps		26	9.5.1943	Bone, Tunisia	
Samuels R.D.	Sergeant	R.A.F.V.R.	Bomber Command	550 Squadron	22	15.3.1944	Nancy, France	
Saville J.	Driver	Army	Royal Army Service Corps		34	11.9.1944	St. Desir, Calvados	
Scott J.A.	Private	Army	Royal Army Service Corps		27	4.6.1945	Salerno, Italy	
Searle C.B.	Firewatcher				39	19.2.1941	Hayes	
Shaw J.C.	Sergeant	R.A.F.V.R.	Bomber Command	49 Squadron POW	23	4.1.1942	Berlin	
Shervill H.J.	Private	Army	Royal Sussex Regiment	2nd. Battalion	28	13.8.1943	Tehran, Iran	
Shewry C.J.	Sergeant	R.A.F.	Bomber Command	144 Squadron	21	22.5.1940	Kleve, Germany	
Simmons S.T.	Chief M.Mech.	Royal Navy	H.M.M.T.B. 278	Motor Torpedo Boat	29	28.6.1943	Calcutta, India	
Simpson C.J.	Corporal	Army	Hampshire Regiment	1/4th. Battalion	24	20.2.1944	Minturno, Italy	
Simpson S	Private	Army	Seaforth Highlanders	7th. Battalion	19	11.7.1944	Bazenville, Calvados	
Simpson W.M.	Craftsman	Army	Royal Artillery		37	8.9.1944	Geel, Antwerp	
Slaughter E.C.	Flight Sergeant	R.A.F.V.R.	Bomber Command	57 Squadron	24	8.2.1945	Helsingborg, Sweden	
Smith E.G.	Lance Corporal	Army	Corps of Military Police		30	28.11.1941	Port Talbot, Glam	
Smith G.F.	Stoker 1st Class	Royal Navy	H.M.S. Fishguard	Coastguard Cutter	19	19.11.1944	Durban, S. Africa	
Smith J.C.	Trooper	Army	Royal Armoured Corps	Warwickshire Yeomanry	21	8.1.1945	Greenford, Middx.	
Smith J.J.	Private	Army	Royal Army Service Corp	208 Petrol Depot POW	40	14.5.1945	Jakarta, Indonesia	

Hayes, Harlington 1939 -1945   Lest We Forget.

Name	Rank	Force	Command	Unit	Age	Date	Place	Where
Smith W.C.	Serjeant	Army	Monmouthshire Regt.	2nd. Battalion	26	19.8.1944	Banneville, Normandy	
Snelling J.	Sapper	Army	Royal Engineers	210 Field Company	32	5.10.1944	Gelderland, Holland	
Spencer P.J.	Pilot Officer	R.A.F.V.R.	Photo Reconaissance	542 Squadron	20	1.12.1943	Botley, Oxon	
Sprake H.W.		Unable to trace						Runnymede
Squibb C.J.	Sergeant	R.A.F.V.R.	Fighter Command	602 Squadron	25	20.9.1941	Eldoret, Kenya	
Stace W.C.	Sergeant	Army	Royal West Kents	8th. Battalion	42	3.12.1942	Cherry Lane, Harlington	
Staples G.F. MBE	Warrant Officer	R.A.F.	R.A.F. Odiham		N/K	4.11.1943	Hermanville, Calvados	
Stevens G.	Private	Army	Seaforth Highlanders	2nd. Battalion	19	28.6.1944	Kanchanaburi, Thailand	
Stevens W.H.	L.A.C.	R.A.F.V.R.	Far East Command	R.A.F. Selectar POW	32	14.7.1943		
Stevenson W.	Private	Army	Lincolnshire Regiment	2nd. Battalion	31	1.6.1940		Dunkirk
Stocker G.H.	Rifleman	Army	Rifle Brigade	2nd. Battalion	29	26.10.1942	El Alamein	
Stokes W.J.	Private	Army	Queens West Surreys	1st. Battalion	20	6.9.1945		Rangoon
Strong G.	Flight Sergeant	R.A.F.V.R.	Bomber Command	96 Squadron	30	25.2.1945	Beverley, Yorks	
Sutcliffe J.	Sergeant	R.A.F.V.R.	Bomber Command	10 Squadron	22	20.6.1943	Bretteville, Calvados	
Swann K.R.	Pilot Officer	R.A.F.V.R.	Bomber Command	6 O.T.U.	26	14.11.1941	Holt, Norfolk	
Sweeting C.R.	Sub-Lieutenant A	R.N.V.R.	H.M.S. Saker	Air Station, Maine, U.S.A.	19	17.2.1945	Long Island, U.S.A.	
Tallack F.H.	Private	Army	Gordon Highlanders	5/7th. Battalion	N/K	5.4.1943	Sfax,Tunisia	
Taplin W.H.	Gunner	Army	Royal Artillery	72 Anti-Tank Regiment	27	19.12.1942	Medjez-el-Bab, Tunisia	
Taylor A	Private	Army	Middlesex Regiment	1st. Battalion POW	21	2.10.1942	Sai Wan, China	
Taylor A. J.	Police Constable			Died at Paddington Station	28	17.4.1941	Cherry Lane, Harlington	
Taylor R.J.	Private	Army	Border Regiment	4th. Battalion	30	20.5.1944	Kohima, Burma	
Thomas C.	Donkeyman	Mechant Navy	SS. Fort Mumford	Steamship	41	20.3.1943		Tower Hill
Thomas E.A.	Corporal	Army	Royal Artillery	attd. 1 (M) A.A. Regt.	38	29.6.1944	Cherry Lane, Harlington	
Thomas S C	Leading Cook	Patrol Service.	H.M.S. Maaloy	Whaler	24	27.3.1944		Lowestoft
Thomas W.E.	Sergeant	R.A.F.V.R.	Bomber Command	149 Squadron	20	30.6.1942	Amsterdam, Holland	
Thompson L.W.	Able Seaman	Royal Navy	H.M.S. Stratagem	Submarine	21	22.11.1944		Chatham
Timms H.	Fire Guard				53	19.2.1944	Cherry Lane, Harlington	
Tod W.	Lance Sergeant	Army	Highland Light Infantry	2nd. Battalion	22	27.3.1945	Florence, Italy	
Topham L.K.	Sergeant	R.A.F.V.R.	Bomber Command	463 Squadron	21	20.2.1944		Runnymede
Tuffin G.A.	Gunner	Army	Royal Artillery	3 Res. Medium Regt.	33	24.8.1946	Hillingdon, Uxbridge	
Turner R.R.	Corporal	Army	Somerset Light Infantry	7th. Battalion	19	27.3.1945	Reichswald, Kleve	
Tyson F.C.	Private	Army	Parachute Regiment	3rd. Battalion	22	26.2.1943	Massicault, Tunisia	

Name	Force	Rank	Command	Unit	Age	Date	Place	Where
Van W.H.	Army	Private	East Surrey Regiment	1st. Battalion	36	17.6.1940		Dunkirk
Waistell J.J.	Army	Lance Corporal	Queen's West Surreys	1/6th. Battalion	33	13.3.1945	Durnbach, Bayern	
Wallis R.A.	Army	Private	Ox. & Bucks Light Inftry.	1st. Battalion	24	19.5.1940	Hainaut, Belgium	
Walton E.	Royal Navy	Signalman	H.M.S. Bedlington		28	5.4.1944	Cherry Lane, Harlington	
Ward L.A.	Army	Driver	Royal Army Service Corp	143 Tank Transport Co.	34	10.5.1945	Soltau, Germany	
Waters E.H.W.	Royal Navy	Chief Artificer	H.M.S. Courageous	Aircraft Carrier	43	17.9.1939		Plymouth
Watts C H.	Army	Private	Royal Scots	2nd. Battalion	20	13.4.1947	Cherry Lane, Harlington	
Watts E.R.	R.A.F. V.R.	Flight Sergeant	Army Co-operation	161 Squadron	23	11.11.1943	St. Desir, Calvados	
Waye R.F.D. DSM	Royal Navy	Ldg. Telegr'phist	H.M.S. Triumph	"T" Class Submarine	24	20.1.1942		Chatham
Weatherhead A.J.	Royal Navy	Ord. Seaman	H.M.S. Soltra	Whaler	25	29.1.1942		Portsmouth
Webb B.J.	Army	Private	Pioneer Corps		37	17.9.1946	Bedfont. Middx.	
West A.F.	R.A.F. V.R.	L.A.C.	35 Wing		24	14.11.1946	Chingford. Essex	
Westcott E.J.	Army	Private	Essex Regiment	1/4th. Battalion	22	18.7.1942	El Alamein	
Wharton A.E.	Army	Private	Pioneer Corps		33	29.9.1945	Cherry Lane, Harlington	
White A.	Army	Rifleman	Rifle Brigade	1st. Battalion	28	20.1.1945	Limburg, Holland	
White A.	Army	Gunner	Royal Artillery		31	29.4.1941	Cherry Lane, Harlington	
White T.	R.A.F.V.R.	Sergeant	Bomber Command	626 Squadron	N/K	1.7.1944	Theillay, Loir-et-Cher	
Whitefield C.F.	R.A.F.V.R.	Sergeant	Bomber Command	463 Squadron	22	25.9.1944		Runnymede
Whitefield L.W.	R.A.F.V.R.	Sergeant	Bomber Command	156 Squadron	27	25.2.1944	Durnbach, Bayern	
Whittle J.	Army	Serjeant	Catering Corps	attd. Royal Artillery	40	1.12.1944		Athens
Wilkins A.L.J.	R.A.F.V.R.	A.C.1.	6570 Servicing Echelon		28	8.6.1944	Harwell, Berks	
Willis F.W.		Civilian			49	1.5.1941	Hayes	
Wilson A.G.L.	Army	Signalman	Royal Corps of Signals	6th. Armoured Division	20	4.11.1944	Cherry Lane, Harlington	
Winter C.A.	R.A.F.V.R.	Sergeant	Bomber Command	35 Squadron	24	24.12.1944	Cherry Lane, Harlington	
Woodger R.G.	Army	Corporal	Royal Corps of Signals		30	6.12.1941	Tobruk, Libya	
Workman R.G.	R.A.F.V.R.	Sergeant	Middle East Airforce	40 Squadron	25	10.11.1942	Heliopolis, Cairo	

MEMORIALS

Below are the details of all the memorials mentioned in this booklet.

ALAMEIN MEMORIAL
The Alamein Memorial commemorates the 8,500 soldiers and 3,000 airmen of the Commonwealth who died in the North African, Middle East, and East African, campaigns and who have no known grave.

ATHENS MEMORIAL
The Athens Memorial stands within Phaleron War Cemetery, and commemorates nearly 3,000 members of the land forces of the Commonwealth who lost their lives in Greece, Crete, the Dodecanese Islands, and Yugoslavia, in World War Two and who have no known grave.

BAYEUX MEMORIAL
The Bayeux Memorial, bears the names of more than 1,800 men of the Commonwealth land forces who died in the early days of the campaign in North-West Europe in 1944, and who have no known grave.

BROOKWOOD MEMORIAL
The Brookwood memorial is situated near Bagshot in Surrey, and commemorates over 3,500 men and women of the land forces who, during the second world war, died at sea, in Norway, and as members of raiding parties or as special agents.

CASSINO MEMORIAL
The Cassino Memorial stands within Cassino War Cemetery and commemorates over 4,000 Commonwealth servicemen who took part on the Italian Campaign, and who have no known grave.

CHATHAM, PORTSMOUTH, & PLYMOUTH MEMORIALS
These three memorials commemorate all seamen who were lost at sea, except the seamen of the Royal Naval Patrol Service who are commemorated at Lowestoft.   Which memorial they are on is determined by the base they were assigned to when they joined the navy   This means that the casualties from one ship can be divided between the three memorials

CHATHAM NAVAL MEMORIAL
The Memorial overlooks the town of Chatham, and commemorates more than 8,500 sailors of the First World War and over 10,000 from the Second World War who have no known grave..

DUNKIRK MEMORIAL.
The Dunkirk Memorial which stands at the entrance to British War Graves section of Dunkirk Town Cemetery commemorates more than 4,500 casualties of British Expeditionary Force who died in the campaign of 1939-40 and who have no known grave.

GROESBEEK MEMORIAL
The Groesbeek Memorial which stands in the Groesbeek Canadian War Cemetery which is located south east of Nijmegen, Holland, and commemorates more than 1000 members the Commonwealth land forces who died during the campaign in north-west Europe between the time of the crossing of the Seine at the end of August, 1944 and the end of the war in Europe, and who have no known grave.

LOWESTOFT NAVAL MEMORIAL
The Naval Memorial is located to the North of the town and is dedicated to the 2,400 men of the Royal Naval Patrol Service who have no grave other than the sea.

MALTA MEMORIAL
The Malta Memorial commemorates 2,400 Commonwealth airmen flying from bases in the Mediterranean and Southern Europe who lost their lives and who have no known grave.
"An Island Resolute in purpose remembers Resolute Men"

MEDJEZ-EL-BAB MEMORIAL
The Medjez-el-Bab Memorial is 60 kms. west of Tunis, and commemorates nearly 2,000 men of the First and Eighth Armies who died in Algeria and Tunis between 8 November 1942 and 13th. May,1943 and who have no known graves.

PLYMOUTH NAVAL MEMORIAL
The Plymouth Memorial is situated centrally on the Hoe, and commemorates 7, 000 sailors from the First World War and 16, 000 from the Second World War, who were lost at sea.

PORTSMOUTH NAVAL MEMORIAL
The Portsmouth Memorial is situated on Southsea Common and overlooks the promenade. It commemorates 10,000 sailors of the First World War, and almost 15,000 from the Second World War, who were lost at sea.

RANGOON MEMORIAL
The Rangoon Memorial bears the names of almost 27,000 men of the Commonwealth land forces who died in Burma (now Myanmar) and who have no known grave.

RUNNYMEDE MEMORIAL
This Runnymede Memorial overlooks the River Thames on Cooper's Hill at Englefield Green between Windsor and Egham on the A.308, 4 miles from Windsor.
It commemorates by name over 20,000 airmen and airwomen who were lost in the Second World War during operations from the United Kingdom and North and Western Europe and who have no known grave.

SAI WAN MEMORIAL
The Sai Wan Memorial is situated in the Sai Wan Cemetery and bears the names of more than 2,000 Commonwealth servicemen who died in the Battle of Hong Kong, or subsequently in captivity, and who have no known grave.

SINGAPORE MEMORIAL
The Singapore Memorial stands in Kranji War Cemetery and bears the names of over 24,000 casualties of the Commonwealth land and air forces who have no known grave.

TOWER HILL MEMORIAL
The Tower Hill Memorial Commemorates the men of the Merchant Navy and Fishing Fleets who died in both world wars and who have no known grave. In the First World War 3,305 Merchant ships were lost with a total of 17,000 men. In the Second 4,786 ships were lost and a total of 32,000 men. This Memorial commemorates 12,000 seaman of the First World War, and 24,000 of the Second.

Bibliography

R.A.F. Squadrons, C. J. Jefford, Airlife Publishing, 1988
Flying Units of the R.A.F, Alan Lake, Airlife Publishing, 1999
R.A.F. Bomber Command Losses of the Second World War, Vol. 1-6, W. R Chorley, Midland Counties Publications. 1992-1997
R.A.F. Fighter Command Losses of the Second World War, Vol. 1-3, Norman L. R. Franks, Midland Counties Publications, 1997
The Right of the Line, John Terraine, Hodder & Stoughton, 1985
Aircrew Unlimited, The Commonwealth Air Training Plan during World War 11, John Golley, PSL, 1999
The Bomber Command War Diaries 1939-1945, Martin Middlebrook and Chris Everitt, 1985
Forgotten Air Force (R.A.F. in the War against Japan 1941-1945) Henry Probert, Brassey, 1995

Companion to the Royal Navy, David Thomas, Harrap, 1987
The Admiralty Regrets, British Warship Losses of the 20th. Century, Kemp, Stroud Sutton 1999
Jane's Fighting Ships of World War 11, Anthony Preston. Bracken Books, 1989
Warship Losses of World War Two, David Brown, Arms and Armour, 1990
Fleet Air Arm Aircraft 1939-1945, Ray Sturtivant with Mick Brown, Air Britain Publications, 1995

Orders of Battle, United Kingdom and Colonial formations and units in the Second World War, Vol. 1 & 2. H.F. Joste, HMSO 1960.
Chasing the Beast, George Grenfield, Richard Cohen Books, 1998.
Sunset of the RAJ, Fall of Singapore, Cecil Lee, Pentland Press, 1994
Singapore, The Pregnable Fortress, P.E.Elphick, 199
Prisoners of the Japanese, Gavan Dawson, Robson Books, 1995
The War North of Rome, June 1944-May 1945, T.Thomas Brooks, Spellmount, 1996
Battleaxe Division, Ken Ford, Sutton, 1999,
War in Italy 1943-1945, Richard Lamb, John Murray. 1993
The Imperial War Museum Book of the War In Italy, Field Marshal Lord Carver, Sidgwick & Jackson, 2001.
World War 11 Day by Day, Anthony Shaw, Military Handbooks 1999
The Struggle for Europe, Chester Wilmot, Wm. Collins 1954
Monty, Master of the Battlefield, 1942-1944, Nigel Hamilton, Hamish Hamilton 1983
And we shall shock them, David Fraser, Hodder & Stoughton, 1983
Monty's Ironsides Patrick Delaforce Chancellor Press 1999
Monty's Highlanders Patrick Delaforce Chancellor Press 2000